Report Number: I33-002R-06

Router Security Configuration Guide Supplement - Security for IPv6 Routers

A supplement to the NSA Router Security Configuration Guide offering security principles and guidance for configuration of IPv6 routers, with detailed instructions for Cisco Systems routers

Router Security Guidance Activity
of the
Systems and Network Attack Center (SNAC)

Author:
Neal Ziring

23 May 2006
Version: 1.0

National Security Agency
9800 Savage Rd. Suite 6704
Ft. Meade, MD 20755-6704

SNAC.Guides@nsa.gov

Warnings

This document is only a guide to recommended security settings for Internet Protocol version 6 (IPv6) routers, particularly routers running Cisco Systems Internet Operating System (IOS) versions 12.3 through 12.4 and 12.4T. It does not provide comprehensive guidance; the directions in this document should be used in conjunction with the NSA Router Security Configuration Guide 1.1c or later. The advice in this document cannot replace well-designed policy or sound judgment. This supplement does not address site-specific configuration issues. Care must be taken when implementing the security steps specified in this document. Ensure that all security steps and procedures chosen from this guide are thoroughly tested and reviewed prior to imposing them on an operational network.

SOFTWARE IS PROVIDED "AS IS" AND ANY EXPRESS OR IMPLIED WARRANTIES, INCLUDING, BUT NOT LIMITED TO, THE IMPLIED WARRANTIES OF MERCHANTABILITY AND FITNESS FOR A PARTICULAR PURPOSE ARE EXPRESSLY DISCLAIMED. IN NO EVENT SHALL THE CONTRIBUTORS BE LIABLE FOR ANY DIRECT, INDIRECT, INCIDENTAL, SPECIAL, EXEMPLARY, OR CONSEQUENTIAL DAMAGES (INCLUDING, BUT NOT LIMITED TO, PROCUREMENT OF SUBSTITUTE GOODS OR SERVICES; LOSS OF USE, DATA, OR PROFITS; OR BUSINESS INTERRUPTION) HOWEVER CAUSED AND ON ANY THEORY OF LIABILITY, WHETHER IN CONTRACT, STRICT LIABILITY, OR TORT (INCLUDING NEGLIGENCE OR OTHERWISE) ARISING IN ANY WAY OUT OF THE USE OF THIS SOFTWARE, EVEN IF ADVISED OF THE POSSIBILITY OF SUCH DAMAGE.

This document is current as of February, 2006. The most recent version of this document may always be obtained through http://www.nsa.gov/.

Acknowledgements

The author would like to thank Casimir Potyraj for his timely and insightful analysis of IPv6 security issues, Ray Bongiorni for technical and structural review, and several external reviewers in industry and government for their technical feedback and suggestions. Thanks also go to the four members of the NSA SNAC that performed the independent quality assurance testing for this guide.

Trademark Information

Cisco and IOS are registered trademarks of Cisco Systems, Inc. in the USA and other countries. Windows is a trademark of Microsoft Corporation.

Revision History

0.1	Aug 2005	Initial outline completed
0.2	Oct 2005	First partial draft
0.3	Dec 2005	Draft more than half complete
0.4	Jan 2006	Draft 2/3 complete, proofreading
0.5.1	Feb 2006	Draft 5/6 complete, internal review
0.6	Mar 2006	Finished draft, QA reviews started
0.7	Apr 2006	Incorporating comments, QA testing begins
0.8	Apr 2006	First external reviews, incorporated comments
0.9	May 2006	Revised after QA testing, ready for pre-pub review
1.0	May 2006	Approved for publication

Contents

List of Figures

Preface

The Internet is entering a period of major transition. The Internet Protocol version 4, which has served the growth of the network for a few dozen hosts to millions, will be gradually replaced by its successor, the Internet Protocol version 6. As networks and devices take on the new responsibilities of IPv6, they will face new risks. During the transition, many routers will support both IPv4 and IPv6 traffic. Further risks may be imposed by the combination of IPv4 and IPv6 support in transitioning networks.

This guide was developed in response to the emerging need for IPv6 security guidance within the US DOD and the US Federal Government. The NSA Systems and Network Attack Center (SNAC) has a long history of providing practical and concrete security guidance, including a widely used security configuration guide for IP routers. That document provides both general and IPv4-specific instructions, but no information specifically about IPv6. This document supplements prior SNAC guidance on router security, providing IPv6-specific recommendations and examples.

The goal for this guide is a simple one: improve the security provided by IPv6 and dual-stack IPv4/IPv6 routers in US Government operational networks.

Who Should Use This Guide

Network administrators and network security officers are the primary audience for this configuration guide. Throughout the text the familiar pronoun "you" is used for guidance directed specifically to them. Most network administrators are responsible for managing the connections within their networks, and between their network and various other networks. Network security officers are usually responsible for selecting and deploying the assurance measures applied to their networks. For this audience, this guide provides security goals and guidance, along with specific examples of configuring Cisco IOS routers to meet those goals.

In particular, this supplement is designed for managers of networks that support both IPv4 and IPv6. Routers have an important role to play in securing such networks, and the guidance given here can help.

Feedback

This guide was created by a small team of individuals in the Systems and Network Attack Center (SNAC), which is part of the NSA Information Assurance Directorate. Comments and feedback about this guide may be directed to the SNAC (Attn: Neal Ziring), Suite 6704, National Security Agency, Ft. Meade, MD, 20755-6704, or via e-mail to *SNAC.Guides@nsa.gov.*

1. Introduction

This section provides an introduction to IPv6 and some of the security issues it poses. Also, this section gives the outline for this supplement, and the relationship between it and the Router Security Configuration Guide (RSCG) version 1.1c [41].

1.1. Overview of IPv6

The IPv6 protocol suite is complex, and described very well in several published books ([1] – [4], [9]) and on-line sources ([10], [39]). This overview introduces a few topics necessary to understand the guidance in Sections 2, 3, and 4.

IPv6 was designed to be both simpler and more flexible than its predecessors. Some of the major differences are listed in the table below. All of these differences have implications for router security configuration.

Property	IPv4	IPv6
Address size and network size	32 bits, network size 8-30 bits	128 bits, network size 64 bits
Packet header size	20-60 bytes	40 bytes (fixed)
Packet-level extensions	limited number of small IP options	unlimited number of IPv6 extension headers
Fragmentation	sender or any intermediate router allowed to fragment	only sender may fragment
Control protocols	mixture of non-IP (ARP), ICMP, and other protocols	all control protocols based on ICMPv6
Minimum allowed MTU	576 bytes	1280 bytes
Path MTU discovery	optional, not widely used	strongly recommended
Address assignment	usually 1 address per host	usually multiple addresses per host

The IPv6 address size was selected to allow for more than enough addresses, and enough extra space to support orderly address assignment and efficient network address aggregation on the Internet.

Basic Terms

The following basic IPv6 definitions are important for any IPv6 discussion.

node   A device on the network that sends and receives IPv6 packets.

router   A node that sends and receives packets, and also accepts packets and forwards them on behalf of other nodes.

host A node that may send and receive packets, but does not forward packets for other nodes.

link A communications medium or channel over which nodes can send and receive IPv6 packets directly (e.g. an Ethernet LAN, an ATM virtual circuit)

interface The point at which a node connects to a link. IPv6 addresses are always associated with interfaces.

1.1.1. Basic IPv6 Packets and Addresses

An IPv6 packet consists of a simple IPv6 header, followed by the packet body or *payload*. The composition of the payload can vary. This sub-section describes the IPv6 header, the structure of an IPv6 packet, and the IPv6 addressing scheme.

The IPv6 Header

The IPv6 header itself is always exactly 40 bytes, and contains exactly 8 fields. Unlike the IPv4 header, the IPv6 header cannot vary in size. The figure below shows the header and explains each of the fields, for details consult RFC 2460 [11].

Version	Traffic Class	Flow Label	
Payload Length		Next Header	Hop Limit
Source Address			
Destination Address			

Version	4 bits, always 6
Traffic Class	8 bits, type of traffic or service
Flow Label	20 bits, identifier for packets in the same flow
Payload Length	16 bits, size of the packet body after the header.
Next Header	8 bits, type of the next protocol header
Hop Limit	8 bits, maximum number of router hops allowed
Source	128 bits, address of sender
Destination	128 bits, address of recipient(s)

Figure 1: The IPv6 Header

Readers familiar with the IPv4 header will immediately notice two major parts of that header absent from the IPv6 header: the checksum field and the fragment fields. The checksum field was simply dropped; all checksum computations in IPv6 must be carried out by upper-layer protocols like TCP and UDP. The fragment fields which appear in the IPv4 header were dropped from the main IPv6 header. Fragment information was relegated to an extension header. Also, IPv6 routers are not allowed to fragment packets they forward; only the original sender of an IPv6 packet is permitted to break the packet into fragments. This has significant implications for network security because ICMP control packets that support path maximum transmission unit (MTU) discovery must be permitted through all IPv6 networks.

Packet Structure

An IPv6 packet consists of the IPv6 header, zero or more extension headers, and the (optional) packet body. Extension headers are a highly flexible mechanism for adding functionality at the network layer, and because they are optional they impose overhead only where they are needed.

The IPv6 header has a field called next header (NH). The NH field always contains the header type of the header immediately following the IPv6 header, whether it is an extension header or a upper-layer protocol header. Each extension header also contains a NH field, which indicates the type of the following header; this is called header chaining. Extension headers that are not fixed in size contain a length field. The last extension header in the packet contains the type of the upper-layer protocol, such as 6 for TCP or 17 for UDP. Figure 2 shows how header chaining works.

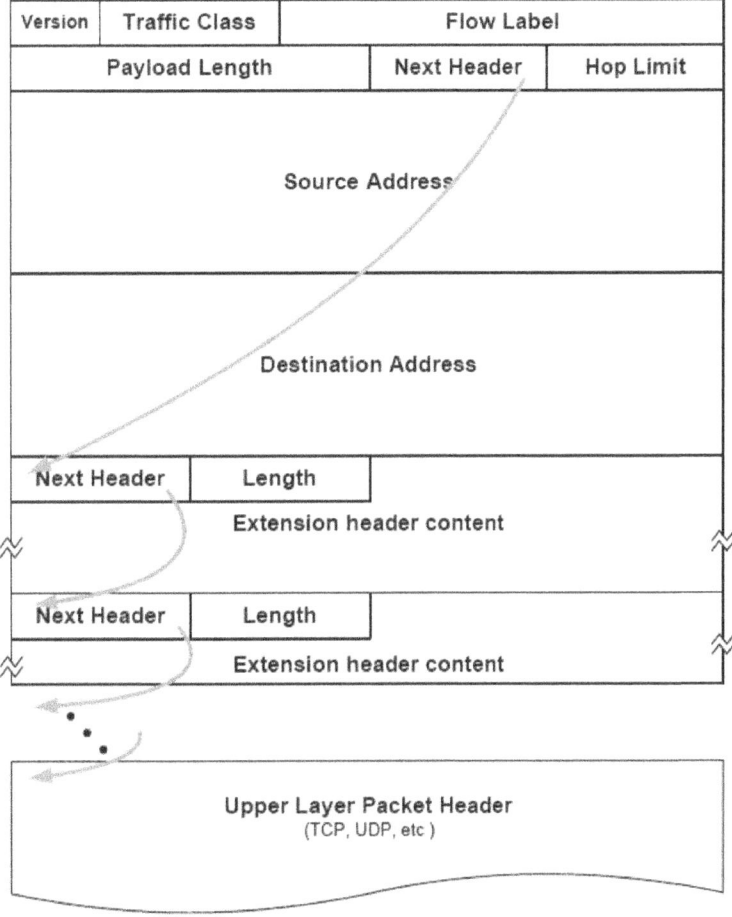

Figure 2: IPv6 Header Chaining

Every extension header and upper-layer protocol has an assigned header type (also sometimes called the protocol number). The table below shows a few of the standard extension header types and payload protocol next header types.

Extension Header	Type	Remarks
Hop-by-Hop Options	0	extension header used for options that apply to intermediate routers
Routing	43	extension header used for source routing
Fragment	44	extension header for fragments, used only by the final recipient
Authentication Header	50	special extension header for IPSec integrity protection (AH)
Encapsulated Security Payload	51	special extension header that precedes an IPSec encrypted payload (ESP)
Destination Options	60	extension header used for options that apply only for the final recipient
Mobility	135	extension header for managing mobile IPv6 bindings

Protocol	Type	Remarks
TCP	6	protocol type, same as IPv4
UDP	17	protocol type, same as IPv4
IPv6-in-IPv6	41	protocol type for IPv6 in IPv6 tunnels
GRE	47	protocol type for Generic Routing Encapsulation tunnels
ICMPv6	58	protocol type, Internet Control Message Protocol for IPv6
no next header	59	special next header value: end of a packet
OSPF	89	protocol type, Open Shortest Path First version 3 routing protocol
PIM	103	protocol type, Protocol Independent Multicast routing
SCTP	132	protocol type, Stream Control Transmission Protocol

IPv6 Addresses

An IPv6 address is 128 bits. Most addresses consist of two parts: the network part and the interface identifier part. Each part is normally 64 bits. The network part, or any leading portion of it, is also called the *prefix*. The structure of the IPv6 address space is defined in RFC 3513 [13] .

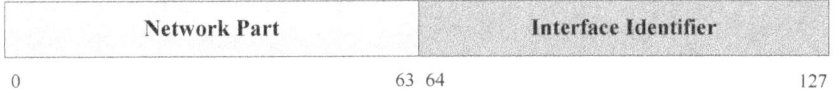

Network Part	Interface Identifier

0   63 64   127

Figure 3: Parts of a Typical IPv6 Address

Addresses are written in hexadecimal, separated into groups of 16 bits: eight groups of four hex digits each, separated by colons.

```
2001:006F:0000:0000:0250:56FF:FEC0:A931
```

Leading zeros can be omitted, and one run of zeros may be replaced with a double colon. The address above can be written as:

```
2001:6F::250:56FF:FEC0:A931
```

Network prefixes are written as an address followed by the prefix length. For example, a network prefix portion of the address above might be:

```
2001:0060::/28
```

Many IPv6 address ranges are reserved or defined for special purposes by the IPv6 standards (set by IETF) and by the Internet Assigned Numbers Authority (IANA). The table below lists the major assignments.

Address Prefix	Assignment or Purpose
`0::1/128`	Loopback address on every interface [RFC 2460]
`0::/96`	Prefix for embedding IPv4 address in an IPv6 address
`2000::/3`	Unicast global address space [RFC 3513]
`2001::/16`	Initial global IPv6 Internet address space [RFC 3056]
`3ffe::/16`	"6Bone" testing assignment (retired, do not use) [RFC 2471]
`fc00::/7`	Unicast unique local address space [RFC 4193]
`fe80::/10`	Link-local address space [RFC 3513]
`fec0::/10`	Site-local address space (deprecated) [RFC 3879]
`ff00::/8`	Multicast address space (see below) [RFC 3513]

Address Types and Scopes

The IPv6 standards define several *scopes* for meaningful IPv6 addresses.

- Interface-local – this scope applies only to a single interface; the loopback address belongs to this scope.

- Link-local – this scope applies to a particular LAN or network link; every IPv6 interface on the LAN must have an address in this scope. Addresses in this scope start with `fe80::/10`. Packets with link-local destination addresses are not routable, and must not be forwarded off the local link.

- Site-local – this scope was intended to apply to all the IPv6 networks of a building, campus, or enterprise. [Site-local addresses are deprecated, and should not be used. Some implementations still support them.]

- Unique local – this scope is meant for site, campus, or enterprise internal addressing. It replaces the deprecated site-local concept. Unique local addresses may be routable within an enterprise. Use of unique local addresses is not yet widespread, see [27] for more information.

- Global – the global scope applies to an entire internet, or the Internet. Packets with global destination addresses are routable.

IPv6 also defines the notion of address *types*:

- Unicast – addresses that uniquely identify one interface on a single node; a packet with a unicast destination address is delivered to that interface.

- Multicast – addresses that identify a group of IPv6 interfaces on one or more nodes; a packet with a multicast destination address will be delivered to all members of the group. Multicast addresses begin with `ff00::/8`.

- Anycast – addresses that identify several interfaces on one or more nodes; a packet with an anycast destination address will be delivered to one of the interfaces bearing the address, usually the closest one.

Multicast addresses are intended for efficient one-to-many and many-to-many communication. The IPv6 standards prohibit sending packets from a multicast address, multicast addresses are valid only as destinations.

Anycast addresses are intended for efficient provision of service where any one of a number of nodes can provide the desired service. At present, anycast addresses may only be assigned to routers, and may not be used as source addresses (see [13]).

IPv4 Compatibility Addresses

The IPv6 standards reserve the 96-bit all-zeros prefix for embedding an IPv4 address in an IPv6 address. This is called a *compatibility address*.

Figure 4: An IPv4 Address Embedded in an IPv6 Address

Compatibility addresses can be written in two ways. For example, the IPv6 address for the IPv4 address 202.87.128.3 can be written in with hex digits or dotted decimal:

```
::ca57:8003          or          ::202.87.128.3
```

When a host's IPv6 stack supports delivering IPv4 packets to programs listening on IPv6 sockets, the source address of the packet will appear to be a compatibility address. Compatibility addresses may be used when a host supports automatic tunnelling of IPv6 packets over IPv4; for more information consult [17].

Multicast Addressing

Multicast is an integral part of IPv6. The address architecture reserves a large chunk of addresses at the top of the address space for multicast, defines some structure for how multicast prefixes are built, and identifies several operationally important multicast addresses. IPv6 does not provide the concept of a broadcast address. All broadcast-like functions are supported by special multicast addresses. The structure of an IPv6 multicast address is shown below.

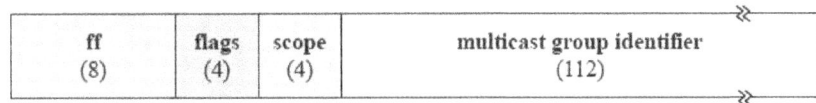

ff (8)	flags (4)	scope (4)	multicast group identifier (112)

Figure 5: IPv6 Multicast Address

There are four values for the scope field that are relevant for this discussion: 2 for link-local, 5 for site-local, 8 for organizational, and 14 (e) for global. The flags field can be used to indicate additional facts about the multicast address, such as whether it is permanently assigned or temporary; for full details consult [11] and [13].

The table below lists some multicast addresses that are relevant for router security.

Multicast Address	Assignment or Purpose
`ff0n::`	reserved all-zeros multicast ID; should never be used (note: reserved for all scope values of n)
`ff02::1`	all-nodes link-local multicast; all interfaces are required to listen to this multicast group
`ff02::2`	all-routers link-local multicast; all routers on a link are required to listen to this multicast group
`ff02::1:ffxx:xxxx`	link-local solicited node multicast; all interfaces with any address ending in $xx:xxxx$ must listen.

1.1.2. Neighbor Discovery, Router Discovery, and Autoconfiguration

To ensure consistent operation of IPv6 on all kinds of communications media, the standards define several control protocols using ICMPv6. For example, in IPv4 the Address Resolution Protocol (ARP) is used for layer 3 to layer 2 address resolution. ARP is not based on IP, is a separate low-level protocol. This is not the case in IPv6 – all control messages for IPv6 are themselves IPv6.

This subsection describes four related control protocols in brief. For full details consult any general IPv6 book (such as [1]-[4]) or the relevant RFCs ([14], [15]). All four of the protocols use ICMPv6 messages.

- Neighbor Discovery (ND) – IPv6 nodes use this protocol to resolve (discover) layer 2 addresses for other IPv6 nodes on the same link. It is analogous to ARP, but more flexible and efficient.

- Router Discovery (RD) – IPv6 hosts can use this protocol to find available routers on the same link; routers use it to advertise their presence and to redirect hosts to more appropriate routers when necessary.

- Stateless Autoconfiguration (autoconf) – When an IPv6 host joins a link, it can use the autoconf procedure and RD protocol messages to select its own addresses based on information from a nearby router.

- Duplicate Address Detection (DAD) – IPv6 nodes use this procedure, and ND protocol messages, to ensure that each of their addresses do not conflict with any address of any other nodes' interfaces on the link.

All four of these protocols use ICMPv6 messages. The table below shows the ICMP message types used. In general, these messages should only traverse the local link, but they must not be blocked because they are essential to correct operation of IPv6 on that link.

ICMPv6 Type	Type Name	Used In	Remarks
133	router solicitation (RS)	RD, autoconf	Query for a nearby router, sent by hosts.
134	router advertisement (RA)	RD, autoconf	Statement by a router about itself and the local link.
135	neighbor solicitation (NS)	ND, DAD	Query about an address, can be sent by any node.
136	neighbor advertisement (NA)	ND, DAD	Statement about an address, can be sent by any node.
137	redirect	RD	Statement sent by a router to direct a node to use a different router on the link.

Collectively, these message types are called "ND/RD messages". If an attacker could inject these messages onto a link, then he could cause several different serious compromises. To prevent this, the IPv6 standards stipulate that all ND/RD messages must be sent with the Hop Limit field set to its maximum value, 255, and that all nodes must ignore ND/RD messages with a Hop Limit less than 255.

While the hop limit restriction prevents attackers from injecting ND/RD messages remotely, there are still significant risks imposed by IPv6 neighbor and router discovery mechanisms. These risks are analogous to the familiar ones posed by ARP and RARP in IPv4 networks, but are magnified by the greater functionality and richness of the IPv6 standards. Unfortunately, these risks cannot be mitigated by router security alone, because they are implicit in the operation of IPv6 networks. Two new IETF standards, SEND and CGA, have been designed to address ND/RD security issues. For more information consult [26] and Section 5.1 (page 108).

Neighbor Discovery

The simplest and most common use of the neighbor solicitation and neighbor advertisement messages is MAC address resolution. In an Ethernet environment, every interface has a vendor-assigned fixed 48-bit MAC address; to send a data packet over Ethernet to a neighboring node, a sender node must discover the neighbor's MAC address.

Figure 6 illustrates the neighbor discovery process at a high level; for details consult RFC 2461 [14].

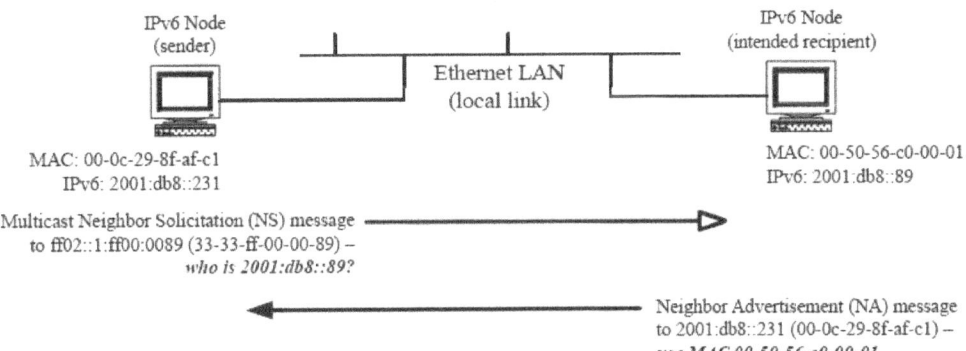

Figure 6: High-level Example of Neighbor Discovery

Note that the sender node knows the IPv6 address it wants to reach, but does not know the MAC address. It must use the link-local solicited-node multicast address to send its neighbor solicitation message, since the desired address is 2001:db8::89, the solicited-node multicast address is ff02::1:ff00:0089. The neighbor solicitation message includes both the IPv6 and MAC addresses of the sender, so the recipient can answer directly (i.e. not using multicast) and supply its own MAC address. The sender can then use the MAC address to send packets directly to the recipient.

Neighbor discovery, and associated procedures like neighbor unreachability detection (NUD) and duplicate address detection (DAD) are absolutely essential to the correct operation of an IPv6 network. It is important to keep this in mind when setting up traffic filtering on router interfaces – if you inadvertently block the ICMPv6 messages used for neighbor discovery, operation of the network will fail.

Router Discovery and Autoconfiguration

IPv6 routers can advertise their services on network links to which they are attached. On each such link, if configured to do so, the router will send router advertisement messages, periodically or in response to router solicitations sent by other nodes. Each router advertisement can contain the following information:

- Default router – whether the router can serve as a default router.

- Router lifetime – how long the router advertisement is valid (usually a few hours, applies only for default routers).
- Prefixes – network prefixes to be used on this link (optional).
- MTU – MTU size to use on this link (optional).
- Timing – neighbor discovery timing information for this link.
- Layer 2 address – link-layer address of the interface to which packets should be sent for routing.
- Flags – flag bits to tell nodes whether to use DHCPv6 for address or other configuration.

Hosts use router advertisements in two situations: during stateless autoconfiguration, and simply to find a default gateway to send packets to addresses that are not on the local link. There is no need to configure a default gateway manually on an IPv6 host; hosts will automatically send router solicitations to find a local router.

Autoconfiguration is an important feature of IPv6. It allows a host to join an IPv6 network and operate as an IPv6 node with no direct administrator input and no dedicated DHCP server. For details of the autoconfiguration process, consult [15]. (Note: DHCPv6 may still be required in many networks, to distribute configuration information beyond addresses, such as DNS information.)

In order for autoconfiguration to work properly, the router sending advertisements must be configured to provide accurate advertisement data. On links where no hosts will be connected, such as backbone or inter-site links, routers should be configured not to send advertisements.

Duplicate Address Detection (DAD)

IPv6 nodes perform DAD before assigning an address to an interface. DAD is designed to prevent two interfaces attached to the same link from claiming the same address. By using neighbor solications messages, a node can determine that an address is already in use on a link, and skip assigning it to an interface on that link. The detailed sequence of steps for DAD are described in [15].

1.1.3. Fragmentation and Path MTU Discovery

IPv6 allows packets up to roughly 64K bytes in size, but popular link layer technologies limit frames to much smaller sizes. Typical Ethernet switches, for example, limit the maximum transmission unit (MTU) to about 1500 bytes. The IPv6 standards require that a link layer must support an MTU of at least 1280 bytes.

Because packets can be larger than the frame size of the links over which they pass, IPv6 defines procedures and an extension header for fragmentation. The original sender of a packet may decide to split it into fragments; each fragment becomes a new IPv6 packet with a fragment extension header. The final recipient reassembles the fragments back into the original packet. Intermediate routers do not fragment packets.

The fragment extension header contains a next header field, an offset (in units of 8 bytes), a 1-bit more-fragments flag, and a 32-bit identification tag. The extension header is shown below.

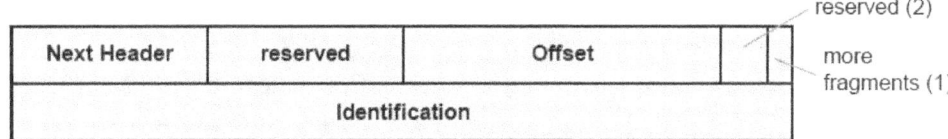

Figure 7: Fragment Extension Header

Conceptually, an IPv6 packet consists of two parts: the unfragmentable part and the fragmentable part. The unfragmentable part consists of the IPv6 header itself, and any extension headers that must be processed by intermediate routers, such as a hop-by-hop options header. The unfragmentable part is replicated on each fragment. The fragmentable part is split across fragments. Each fragment payload (except the last one) must be a multiple of 8 bytes in length. The offset field in each fragment header indicates the offset of that fragment from the beginning of the original payload, in units of 8 bytes. Figure 8 shows how an example packet would be fragmented.

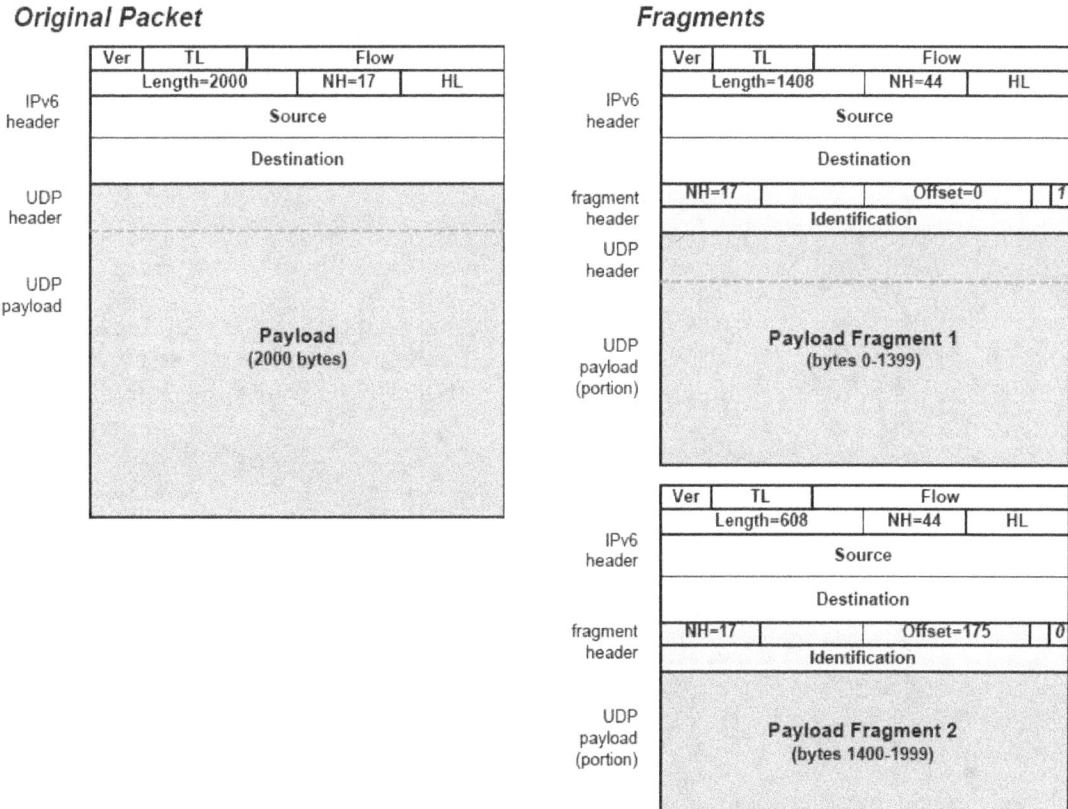

Figure 8: Simple Example of IPv6 Fragmentation

Path MTU Discovery

In IPv4, the original sender or any intermediate router could fragment packets. IPv6 does not permit this; only the original sender of an IPv6 packet is allowed to break it into fragments. Therefore, if a router receives a packet that is too big to be forwarded along the necessary link, it must send a Packet-too-big ICMPv6 error message back to the original sender. This message informs the sender that (a) the original packet was dropped, and (b) that it must be re-sent in smaller fragments.

The IPv6 standards specify a mechanism for nodes to discover the maximum packet size (transmission unit) that can traverse the entire path from the sender to the final recipient: path MTU discovery (PMTUD, see [16]). The PMTUD procedure depends on receiving Packet-too-big messages from intermediate routers.

Because the original sender is the only node permitted to fragment a packet, and because ICMPv6 messages indicate when fragmentation is necessary, IPv6 routers must permit ICMPv6 messages to pass. It is not practical to reject all ICMPv6 messages at border routers or other intermediate points, as you might for IPv4.

1.1.4. Transition Mechanisms

The IETF intends for the migration from IPv4 to IPv6 to be slow, gradual, and especially not disruptive. To this end, the IPv6 standards define several transition mechanisms intended to support co-existence between IP versions and network users that migrate at different rates. For more details, see [1], [2], [9] and RFC 4213 [17].

There are three main kinds of transition mechanisms.

1. Dual-Stack Operation –
   hosts and routers can support both IPv4 and IPv6 traffic simultaneously. Dual-stack can be important for reaching Internet resources accessible using only one protocol or the other. Figure 9 illustrates this concept.

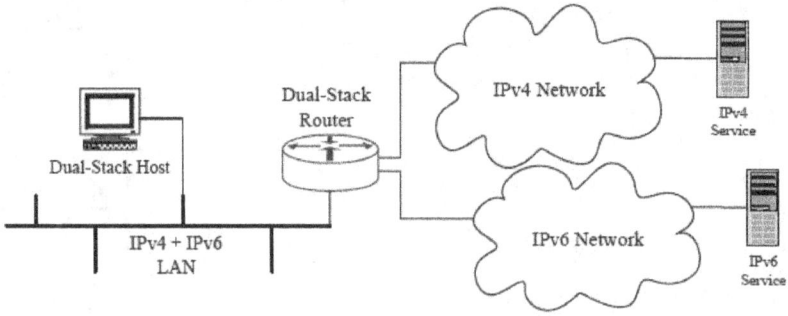

Figure 9: IPv4/v6 Dual-Stack Operation

2. Encapsulation –
   sites that support IPv6 can communicate to other IPv6 nodes over the IPv4 Internet by encapsulating the IPv6 packets in IPv4 packets; this is

called *tunneling*. This mechanism is important for linking IPv6 networks over existing IPv4 infrastructure. It is also possible to tunnel IPv4 packets over IPv6 networks. Figure 10 illustrates a simple IPv6 over IPv4 tunnel between two routers.

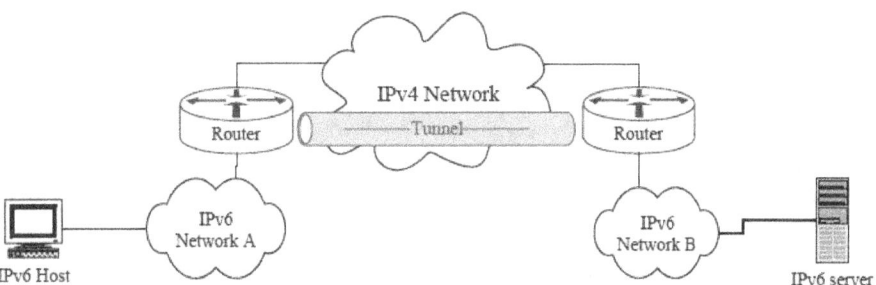

Figure 10: An IPv6 Tunnel Across an IPv4 Network

Tunnels can be configured manually on most IPv6 hosts and routers, and several standard mechanisms for automatic tunneling are defined. Security for manual tunnels is covered in Sections 3.5 and 4.2.3. You can get more information about tunnels from [2], [5], [17], and [42].

3. Translation –
hosts and networks that use only IPv6 can employ translation at their connection to the IPv4 Internet; a translation mechanism can convert traffic between IPv4 and IPv6 to allow application interoperability. (This is analogous to IPv4 Network Address Translation.) There are several translation specifications, the most mature is NAT-PT [31].

This supplement provides security advice for routers configured for dual-stack operation (supporting both IPv4 and IPv6 concurrently), and for setting up certain kinds of tunnels. Translation mechanisms are not covered in this supplement.

1.2. Motivations for IPv6 Router Security

An IPv6 network will have different security concerns and face different security risks than an IPv4 network. As discussed in Convery and Miller's IPv4/v6 threat comparison [38], the larger address space of IPv6 discourages attacks based on address scanning, but many other kinds of traditional IPv4 attacks are still viable. Operational requirements of IPv6 impose their own risks, and thus require different security responses from network administrators. Networks that carry both IPv4 and IPv6 traffic, so-called dual-stack or mixed networks, face risks from both protocols and additional potential risks from combinations of them. Section 2 covers some of the threats in more detail.

Today, many enterprises depend on their networks for critical operations. The US Government and US Department of Defense (DOD) depend on IP networks for every aspect of their operations. The US Government has already committed to supporting IPv6 on its backbone networks by 2008. Many commercial network service providers already support IPv6, and offer IPv6 connectivity to their customers. In many cases, enterprises support IPv6 in their network infrastructure first, and then begin supporting it with various hosts and servers. In other cases, enterprises experiment with isolated pilot networks running IPv6, and then enable IPv6 support in the infrastructure. In both cases, routers serve an important role in enforcing enterprise security policies on network traffic.

Routers have a critical role in protecting our networks during the transition from IPv4, through mixed IPv4/v6 networks, to future IPv6 networks. Configured properly, a router can protect itself from attacks over IPv6, and can also protect the networks it serves. If many IPv6 network administrators apply the same protections consistently, then that will help ensure predictable and reliable IPv6 service.

1.3. Relation to the NSA Router Security Configuration Guide

The NSA RSCG 1.1 provides extensive guidance for configuring Cisco IOS routers securely. It deals with general issues related to authentication, integrity, and availability, and it provides specific instructions for configuring many IOS network features. The specific instructions cover IPv4 only. The same security principles apply for IPv4, IPv6, and mixed networks, but the particular concerns and specific IOS commands are very different for IPv4 and IPv6.

This supplement extends the general principles discussed in the RSCG 1.1 to IPv6. It also presents some specialized concerns, and instructions for addressing them, that can arise in mixed IPv4/v6 networks. This supplement is not meant to stand alone; a router locked down using only the instructions here would not be secure. Instead, this supplement has been written assuming that the routers of concern have already been secured using the guidance in the RSCG or a similar general guide.

For a router operating in dual-stack mode, both IPv4 guidance and IPv6 guidance should be applied before putting the router into operational use. Guidance on securing IPv4 routers may be found in several books (such as [6] and [8]), in the original RSCG [41], and in the DISA Network Infrastructure Security Technical Information Guide (STIG) [57].

1.4. Structure of this Document

The body of this supplement is divided into three parts. Section 2 describes some IPv6 security issues that routers face, including the role of a router in an IPv6 network, and some of the threats routers can help to mitigate. Section 3 covers basic IPv6 security, including interface configuration, packet filtering, configuring tunnels, and viewing IPv6 status information. Section 4 presents some advanced IPv6 topics: security for routing protocols, setting up IPSec for IPv6 and IPv6 tunnels, and using the IOS Firewall. Section 5 describes two emerging issues that will probably affect secure IPv6 router configuration in the near future.

2. IPv6 Security Issues for Routers

This section presents some security concerns that must be addressed when deploying IPv6, particularly issues that affect the configuration and operation of routers.

This supplement does not cover general security policy for routers. The basic structure of the security policy will be the same for IPv4, IPv6, or a mix of the two. Consult section 3.4 of the RSCG ([41]) for a short discussion of security policy.

2.1. The Roles of a Router Serving an IPv6 Network

An IPv6 router provides many functions to support the operation of an IPv6 network. The list below describes some of the functions and roles an IPv6 router must fill. When securing a router, you seek to assure the integrity and availability of these functions.

- Every IPv6 router must satisfy the requirements of an IPv6 node: perform neighbor discovery, listen on various multicast addresses, process certain extension headers, etc. (see [11], [14], and [15]). Routers also have the responsibility for parsing designated hop-by-hop extension headers.

- Besides neighbor discovery, a router must also support router discovery.

- An IPv6 router must be capable of forwarding unicast, multicast, and anycast traffic.

- As part of its support for multicast, an IPv6 router must also support Multicast Listener Discovery (MLD, see [18], and MLDv2, see [19]).

- To support scalable and dynamic routing, IPv6 routers usually support one or more routing protocols, such as RIPng, OSPF version 3, and others.

- In practice, routers must often filter or selectively forward traffic; IPv6 routers should be able to do this based on source and destination address, protocol, and many other attributes. Routers should be able to support traffic engineering or quality-of-service (QoS) goals.

- During the transition from IPv4 to IPv6, routers will provide interoperability and co-existence between the two protocols. In particular, dual-stack routers must be able to serve IPv4 and IPv6 networks, provide tunnels, and perform translation.

- The IPv6 standards mandate support for IPSec. IPv6 routers should be able to employ IPSec to provide integrity and confidentiality assurance for traffic between networks.

In networks where IPv4 and IPv6 are in use, routers must be able to forward, filter, and restrict IPv6 packets independently of IPv4 packets.

2.2. Basic Threats and Countermeasures

The most fundamental threat for routers is physical. If an attacker can gain physical access to your router, they can compromise the availability, integrity, or even the confidentiality of your network and its traffic. To reduce the risk from physical access attacks, keep operational routers in locked rooms accessible only to authorized personnel. If availability of the router or the networks it serves is particularly important, install an uninterruptible power supply (UPS) and keep spare components and parts on hand.

We can characterize network threats to routers and their networks by *plane*. Each plane provides different services, and thus exposes the router to different threats.

Plane	Description	Typical Protocols
management plane	Services and settings that support administration of the router, including user authentication and access control, configuration, and software updates.	Telnet, SSH, FTP, RADIUS, SNMP, TACACS+
control plane	Services, settings, and data streams that support the dynamic operation, and traffic handling of the router. The control plane includes logs, routing protocols, and cryptographic negotiations.	RIP, OSPF, IS-IS, EIGRP, BGP, NTP, Syslog, IKE, MLD, SNMP
data plane	Services and settings related to data passing through the router among the networks it serves. The data plane includes packet forwarding, QoS assurance, traffic conversion (e.g. tunnels and encryption), and traffic filtering.	TCP, UDP, ICMP, IPv4, IPv6, ICMPv6

Figure 11, below, illustrates the different planes.

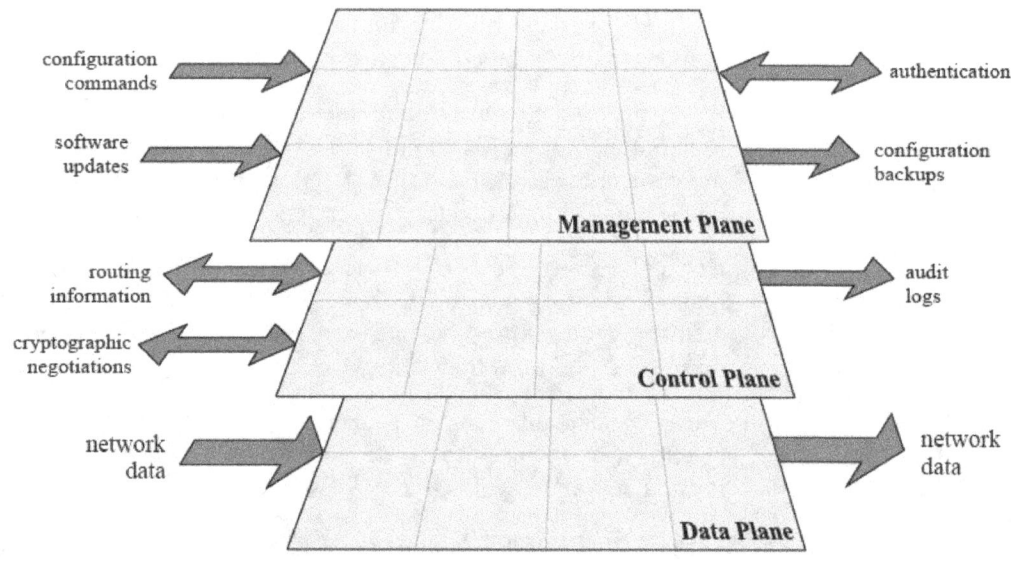

Figure 11: Three-Plane View of Router Operations

Threats to the management plane can affect the long-term configuration of the router, and thus all aspects of its operation. For example, remote administration is part of the management plane. If an attacker can gain remote administrative read access, they can examine the configuration and operation of the router, and deduce a great deal about the networks it serves. If an attacker can gain fully privileged administrative access, they can compromise the availability, integrity, and confidentiality of your network.

The control plane supports the dynamic state of the router: the routing tables, access logs, traffic statistics, and cryptographic associations. All of these depend on protocols and network data exchange with management tools, network hosts, and other routers. The key security objective for control information is usually integrity, but the integrity of control information can affect the confidentiality and availability of your networks. If an attacker can inject control plane information into your router, then they can exercise some control over packet forwarding, expose traffic to intercept, and prevent effective communication among networks and hosts. Effective incident detection and response may rely on the integrity of audit logs and traffic statistics. Neighbor and router discovery are part of the control plane; by compromising them an attacker can deny service or redirect traffic on the local link.

The data plane supports transit traffic. A router is responsible for using management and control plane information to forward traffic correctly, to filter and rate-limit traffic, and to provide encapsulation and encryption services for traffic. In these roles, a router helps ensure integrity, confidentiality, and availability for the networks it serves. Router packet filtering is often a key mechanism enforcing security policies about what kinds of traffic can enter or leave a network. Accurate forwarding is essential for network availability. If an attacker can bypass or defeat the security controls on the data plane, they can gain greater access to the networks that the router protects.

Overall, a secure router configuration applies safeguards on all three planes to defend the router itself and the networks it serves.

2.3. IPv6-Specific Threats and Countermeasures

This sub-section describes some specific router security threats to IPv6 and mixed IPv4/v6 networks, and identifies general countermeasures for mitigating them.

Administration and Management Threats

IPv6 and dual-stack routers face all the same threats to administration and management as a IPv4 routers. The key issue to remember is that IPv6 provides a separate, independent channel for communicating with your router, and all the protections you would normally apply to management must be imposed for IPv6, too.

> **Threat:** Unauthorized remote management via IPv6 connections.
> **Countermeasures:** Impose access controls that explicitly cover IPv6.

Discussion: Most routers support a variety of remote management protocols, some examples include Telnet, SSH, HTTP, HTTPS, and SNMP. All of these protocols can work over IPv6. It is essential to impose access control and authentication for every remote management facility on your router.

Threat: Window of vulnerability during IPv6 configuration.

Countermeasures: Configure and apply IPv6 safeguards on management, control, and data planes before enabling IPv6 on interfaces.

Discussion: It is important to prepare your router for potential attacks <u>before</u> exposing it on the network. When first connecting a new IPv6 router, or when adding IPv6 capabilities to an existing router, set up safeguards before allowing the router to process or accept any IPv6 traffic. Connecting your router before configuring security will leave a gap during which attackers could compromise the device.

Threat: Disclosure of information about router addresses, settings, and status to unauthorized parties.

Countermeasures: Disable or restrict services that can provide attackers with information about the router and its connected networks, use loopback interfaces to bind router services to addresses that are not visible on the forwarding path, and set non-obvious static addresses on all router interfaces.

Discussion: Only authorized network administrators and managers have the need to know how your routers are configured and operating. Prevent exposure of sensitive information about your routers by disabling or imposing access controls on all relevant services. For example, the ICMPv6 node information query message can be used to probe routers; disable responses to node information queries. Attackers can always discover the addresses of transit interfaces by using *traceroute*; avoid using these addresses for router services, use static addresses assigned to a loopback interface instead. Lastly, the large address space of IPv6 makes scanning impractical, but attackers can guess important router addresses by assuming that you've chosen obvious addresses (avoid choices like `2001:db8::1`). Devise a scheme for assigning hard-to-guess router addresses and use it. Also, ensure that addresses on transit interfaces and on loopbacks do not match up.

Most management plane safeguards that apply to IPv4 also apply to IPv6. For more information about router management plane safeguards, consult [6], [8], [41], [57], and their many references.

Control Plane Threats

IPv6 networks depend on several control protocols, and can use a variety of routing protocols. Router operations depend on several additional protocols and services. All of these must be configured securely or disabled.

Threat: Traffic routed incorrectly, dropped, or exposed to intercept by unauthorized parties.

Countermeasures: Ignore unauthorized network redirects, protect integrity of routing protocols, and authenticate routing protocol peers.

Discussion: The integrity of the forwarding table and the neighbor cache are very important to secure router operations. Redirects and other neighbor discovery attacks can corrupt the neighbor cache. Route injection attacks can corrupt the forwarding table. Routers may send redirects, but typically should not accept them. Routing protocols should be protected with authentication and integrity measures to ensure that each router accepts routing updates only from authorized peers.

Threat: Router services degraded by attacks that consume router resources like memory, control plane bandwidth, or computation capacity.

Countermeasures: Impose strict timeouts and rate-limiting on control protocols, and disable protocols on interfaces where they are not needed.

Discussion: Do not let attackers consume excessive router resources, such attacks can degrade service for legitimate users, or cause the router to miss routing updates. IPv6 rate-limiting, especially rate-limiting at the control plane, can be effective in suppressing such attacks.

Threat: Untrustworthy audit logs due to inaccurate timestamps and missing log entries.

Countermeasures: Configure redundant network time servers to ensure reliable time synchronization, and use NTP integrity protection to prevent malicious attacks against the router's clock.

Discussion: Accurate and precise timestamps are essential for good audit logs, especially log analyses that correlate events at multiple network devices. It's also important for time synchronization to be reliable; each router should have at least a primary and backup source of time configured.

Threat: Modification of router state, including routing tables, traffic filters, and addresses, by unauthorized parties.

Countermeasures: Disable or protect all network services and protocols that allow changing router state.

Discussion: Some protocols, notably SNMP, support reading and writing portions of the router's state. SNMP and other protocols can run over IPv4 or IPv6. These protocols should be disabled when possible, and otherwise subjected to strict access control, confidentiality, and integrity protections.

Some control plane services can be turned off, but many of them are essential to router operations. Protect the services that you must run, using access controls, authentication, and confidentiality measures like encryption.

The list above covers only threats that have facets specific to IPv6. Additional discussion of control plane threats and countermeasures may be found in [6], [9], [39], and [41]. RFC 3756 offers an excellent discussion of specific threats to IPv6 link-local control protocols [26].

Data Plane Threats

The data plane is where traffic flows through the router, rather than specifically to or from the router. IPv6 and IPv4/v6 transition mechanisms can pose numerous risks for networks, and routers can help mitigate them.

All routers must be configured to protect their own management and control planes. While data plane threats exist for all IPv6 networks, not all routers need to apply countermeasures for those threats. Carefully consider the security role that each router has in your network, and apply data plane security controls accordingly. For example, a transit router that carries traffic among several equally trusted networks may not need to filter out unauthorized traffic – that job could be relegated to a bastion router at the enterprise boundary.

Threat: Unauthorized parties attempting to probe or map the networks that the router serves.

Countermeasures: Reject, restrict, or rate-limit incoming packets that can be used for mapping, most notably some ICMPv6 messages. Drop or rate-limit outgoing packets that can expose network structure unnecessarily.

Discussion: For border routers at the edge of enterprise networks, it is especially important to control inappropriate probes coming into the enterprise, and injudicious responses leaving the enterprise. Some of the same protocols that can be used to conduct illicit probing and mapping are also required for proper operation of IPv6 networks; therefore, it is not practical to block them completely.

Threat: Unauthorized traffic types or protocols crossing between networks.

Countermeasures: Filter traffic entering the router. Reject or drop unauthorized traffic where possible.

Discussion: For border or bastion routers, and any router that connects networks with different security postures, traffic filtering can be an essential mechanism for enforcing security policy. There are two primary approaches to filtering:

- Deny-then-allow: reject specific unauthorized traffic, and allow everything else. This requires that the security policies define what protocols or messages are prohibited from crossing the router.

- Allow-then-deny: allow specific authorized traffic, and deny everything else. This requires that security policies enumerate the permitted protocols and messages.

The second approach, denying all traffic except what is explicitly permitted, usually provides tighter security at the cost of reduced convenience.

Threat: traffic with spoofed or invalid source addresses crossing between networks.

Countermeasures: drop all packets with inappropriate source addresses, and consider logging or counting such packets.

Discussion: Fake source addresses are never a good thing, and any packets whose source address can be confirmed as fake should be dropped by the router. The IPv6 standards define certain addresses that are invalid to use as source addresses (e.g. multicast), and any packet with such a source address should also be dropped. Also, obviously spoofed addresses should be rejected, according to the principles documented in RFC 2827 [24].

Threat: IPv6 traffic crossing IPv4 networks in unauthorized IPv4 tunnels.

Countermeasures: Drop encapsulated packets except when they are part of authorized tunnels. Drop control packets for automated tunnel mechanisms, unless those mechanisms are explicitly authorized.

Discussion: Tunnels are a powerful transition mechanism that must be employed with care. During the transition from IPv4 to IPv6, many enterprises will use tunnels to connect separated IPv6 networks over existing IPv4 infrastructure. Tunnel facilities should be explicitly authorized by responsible management, and configured by trained network administrators. Prohibit ad hoc tunnels set up by users, and configure the router to drop unauthorized tunnel packets. (Malicious users can still hide traffic with encrypted protocols like SSH and SSL, but good filtering is useful in defeating automatic tunnels that some hosts may attempt to create.)

Threat: Unauthorized parties injecting IPv6 traffic into enterprise networks through authorized IPv4 tunnels.

Countermeasures: Protect operational tunnels with confidentiality, integrity, and authentication mechanisms.

Discussion: Bare IPv6-over-IPv4 tunnels do not prevent attackers on the IPv4 network from injecting packets via the tunnel, as illustrated below.

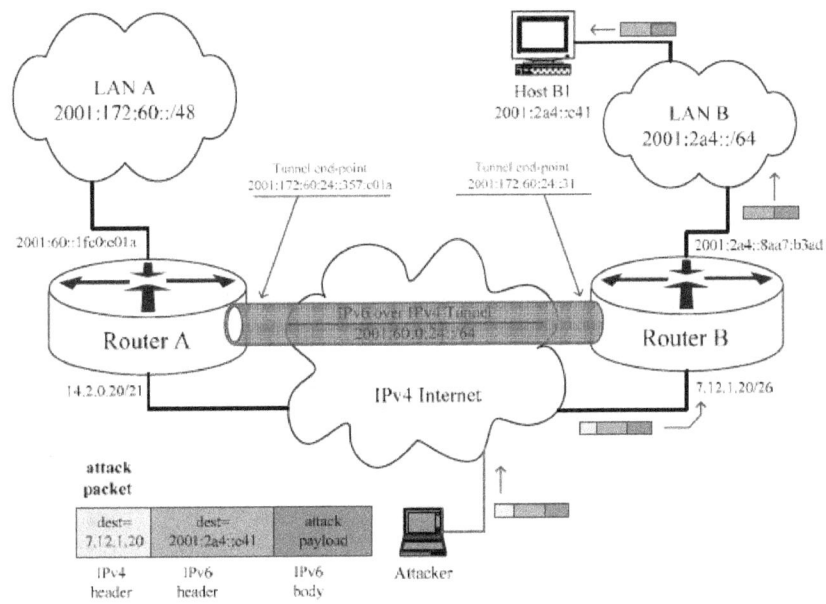

Figure 12: Traffic Injection via a Tunnel

As the security community gains more experience with IPv6, new threats may emerge. Mobile IPv6, in particular, has not yet been widely deployed; threats for it are not yet fully understood. RFC 3755 [36] identifies some security concerns and includes several references.

For some additional discussion of IPv6 network threats, consult Chapter 9 of the 6Net IPv6 deployment guide [10], and the Convery and Miller threat paper [38].

3. Basic IPv6 Security for IOS Routers

This section describes some fundamental IPv6 settings and facilities for Cisco IOS routers. It begins with a brief discussion of which IOS releases support IPv6, and how to check whether your router is IPv6-capable. The following sub-sections cover initial IPv6 configuration, IPv6 traffic filtering and policing, and configuring IPv6-over-IPv4 tunnels.

This section does not provide general guidance for deploying IPv6 in your network; for that consult one of the many books on IPv6 operations, such as [5], [7], or [9].

3.1. Obtaining IPv6-Capable Cisco IOS Releases

If your router is not yet handling IPv6 traffic, it may not be obvious whether it is suitable for operational IPv6. Most Cisco router chassis, except some older models, can support an IPv6-capable IOS; the usual issue is whether a particular router has enough memory (RAM and Flash) to load and run a particular IOS release.

Many recent IOS releases support IPv6; the table below shows a rough list of them.

IOS Version	IPv6 Capabilities	Remarks
12.0S	Full IPv6 support on a few router models.	Certified only on the high-end 12000 model.
12.2S, 12.2T	Incomplete IPv6 support in some editions, full support in others. Need 12.2(2)T or later.	Suitable for lab testing. For operational use, consider 12.3 or 12.4 instead.
12.3, 12.3T	Full support for IPv6 in many editions, 12.3T offers additional features and capabilities.	Suitable for operational use after testing. Certified for a wide array of router models.
12.4, 12.4T	Full support for IPv6 in many editions.	Suitable for operational use after testing.

Within each major version number (e.g. 12.3) there are point releases (e.g. 12.3.15). Each release is available for a wide array of different hardware chassis, and in several different feature packages: IP Base, Advanced Security, Enterprise, etc. The mix of features supported on a particular IOS image can depend on all of these things. (Cisco offers the Feature Navigator and Software Advisor tools at their web site to help you find the right edition for your hardware. These tools require a Cisco CCO account to use.) Any IOS release 12.3 and later marked "Advanced IP Services" or "Advanced Enterprise Services" will have substantial IPv6 support; for more information use the Feature Navigator or consult [43], [46] and [47].

If you have administrative access to a router, it is relatively easy to check whether it supports IPv6 at all. Type the command `show ipv6 ?` and examine the output; an

IPv6-capable IOS release will show a list of commands, but a non-IPv6-capable release will report an input error. The two transcripts below show the difference.

```
cat1# show ipv6 ?
% Unrecognized command
cat1#
```

versus

```
North# show ipv6 ?
  access-list  Summary of access lists
  cef          Cisco Express Forwarding for IPv6
  interface    IPv6 interface status and configuration
    .
    .
  tunnel       Summary of IPv6 tunnels
North#
```

You can also use the `show version` command to see the exact IOS version and release number.

If you need IPv6 but your router's current IOS image does not support it, obtain a newer or more capable IOS release from Cisco. If you have not been instructed to use a particular version and release, use the Feature Navigator to select the correct image for your operational or testing needs. Check carefully for specialized requirements that apply to many Cisco router models, such as minimum memory size and firmware version. Use the *md5sum(1)* utility and MD5 checksum published at the Cisco web site to validate that the images you download have not been corrupted.

Installing a new IOS image onto a Cisco router requires shutting down the router and taking it out of service for *at least* several minutes, and potentially much longer if the new image fails to boot. To be conservative, assume that the router may be out of service for up to an hour. When installing a new image, always follow the steps listed below. It is always safest to perform IOS installations from the console, because if the reboot at step 6 fails, it may be impossible to reconnect remotely.

1. Check the current IOS version and image name using the command `show version`. Check to make sure that the router has enough RAM to run the new IOS image you are about to install. Check the available Flash memory space using the command `show flash`.

2. Copy the current IOS image and startup configuration to a secure host. These are your backups in case the installation fails and your need to roll back. (Use the SCP protocol if possible, otherwise use FTP. Avoid TFTP unless the router's IOS is so old that it supports nothing else.)

3. Download the new image using the `copy` command.

4. Remove any boot specifications that point to the old image, using the `no boot system imagename` command.

5. Disable all interfaces, then save the running configuration.

6. Reboot the router using the command `reload`.

7. Watch the router boot, taking note of any error messages. When the router comes up, check that critical addresses, interface settings, and routing protocol configurations were correctly applied.

8. Enable interfaces, then save the running configuration.

The capsule description above provides enough detail for experienced Cisco router administrators. Section 4.5 of the Router Security Configuration Guide [41] provides a detailed description of essentially the same procedure, with a transcript.

3.2. Initial Configuration

The diagram below shows a simple mixed IPv6 network. This network will be used for most of the examples in Sections 3 and 4.

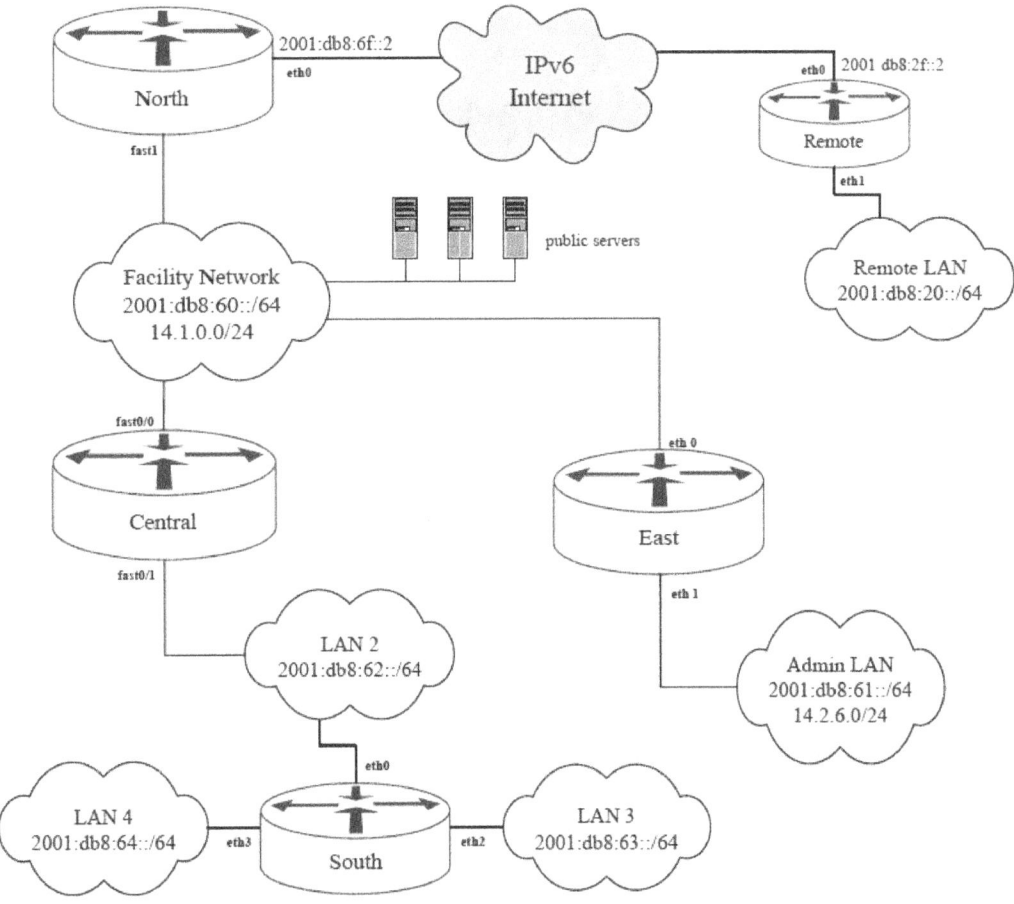

Figure 13: Network to be Used for Examples

Order of Steps

Follow this general principle when performing initial IPv6 configuration on connected routers: apply safeguards and access restrictions <u>before</u> permitting traffic. By default, most network services offered by IPv6-capable IOS routers will be accessible via IPv6 at the moment you assign an IPv6 address to any interface. Ensure that all services are either disabled or covered by access restrictions before you activate IPv6.

The detailed descriptions below show you how to set up simple IPv6 routing support on Cisco IOS 12.3 and later, laying the foundations for good security. The general sequence is given below.

Before you begin, select two random numbers, P1 and P2, for each router. These will be the private interface ID numbers for your router: P1 will be used for interfaces that handle transit traffic, and P2 will be used only for the loopback interface. Each number should be 6-8 hex digits. Using these private numbers will make it more difficult for potential attacks to probe your router during network scans (see p. 23).

1. Set up and apply remote access restrictions for all remote administration services.

2. For each interface that will support IPv6, perform the following:

    * set up IPv6 address(es),
    * set up and apply simple packet filtering,
    * disable unneeded network services, and
    * adjust router discovery and stateless autoconfiguration settings.

3. Enable IPv6 forwarding and enable IPv6 processing on each interface.

This section assumes that your router is already configured securely for general use and management with IPv4. If that is not true, consult Chapter 4 of the RSCG [41].

The detailed configuration examples below show the initial setup steps for the router Central. For Central, we've chosen P1 = f14b:65a1 and P2 = ee15:f00d.

3.2.1. Initial Setup Part 1: Restrict Remote Management

First, ensure that IPv6 will not open illicit means for attackers to remotely probe and administer your router. Every remote management service should be either disabled and/or protected with an IPv6 access list.

For each such service, create and apply an IPv6 access list restricting access to the router's remote management services. For services that are not authorized for use in your network, apply an access list that prevents all access, and also ensure that the service is disabled. (For information about disabling services, see Section 4.2 of the RSCG [41] or Section 3.4.4 of the DISA Network Infrastructure STIG [57].)

It is important to create and apply the access list <u>before</u> commencing IPv6 operation. Even if the router has been configured to prohibit remote administrative access, you should still create and apply these restrictions. The example below shows how to create an access list that permits access from the Admin LAN and the Facility LAN. The end of the example shows how to apply the access list and how to restricting access to Telnet and SSH only. (Section 3.3 gives information on IPv6 access lists.)

```
Central# config t
Enter configuration commands, one per line. End with CNTL/Z
Central(config)# no ipv6 access-list remote-mgmt-acl
Central(config)# ipv6 access-list remote-mgmt-acl
Central(config-ipv6-acl)# remark allow login only to loopback0
Central(config-ipv6-acl)# permit tcp 2001:db8:61::/64
                         host 2001:db8:6f::ee15:f00d log-input
Central(config-ipv6-acl)# permit tcp 2001:db8:60::/64
                         host 2001:db8:6f::ee15:f00d log-input
Central(config-ipv6-acl)# deny ipv6 any any log-input
Central(config-ipv6-acl)# exit
Central(config)# line vty 0 4
Central(config-line)# ipv6 access-class remote-mgmt-acl in
Central(config-line)# transport input ssh telnet
Central(config-line)# exit
Central(config)#
```

The access list shown above permits remote administration connections only to the loopback interface, and only from hosts on the 2001:db8:61::/64 or 2001:db8:60::/64 networks. The access list generates log entries for all connection attempts.

The command `ipv6 access-class` applies the access list to designated remote management VTY lines. Operationally, all VTY lines should be protected in this fashion. To check how many VTY lines your router supports, use the command `show line vty 0 100`. For more information about VTY lines, check section 4.1.5 of the RSCG [41].

3.2.2. Initial Setup Part 2: Configure Interfaces

Next, configure IPv6 on each interface that must support it. There are three important aspects of the configuration to consider:

- The addresses for the interface: assign each interface an address from the network supported on its connected link. It is not necessary to assign a link-local address, IOS automatically creates a link-local address for each interface supporting IPv6.

- Router advertisements: configure router advertisements on each interface, along with parameters, to support stateless autoconfiguration. For network backbone links, networks where hosts will not be attached, or networks where the router will not be a default gateway, suppress advertisements.

- Disable unneeded IPv6 interface services. For example, disable redirects if they are not needed on a particular link.

Router global unicast addresses should be statically configured, but should not be trivially guessed values like "::1" or "::ffff". Do not make it easy for potential remote attackers to probe your router's interface. Instead, assign a difficult-to-guess value of at least 6 hex digits for each router, and use that value as the basis for global addresses on interfaces.

For the router Central, we will configure addresses on two FastEthernet interfaces, using P1 for the interface ID.

```
Central# config t
Enter configuration commands, one per line. End with CNTL/Z
Central(config)# interface fast0/0
Central(config-if)# description Link for facility LAN
Central(config-if)# ipv6 address 2001:db8:60::f14b:65a1/64
Central(config-if)# exit
Central(config)# interface fast0/1
Central(config-if)# description Link for LAN 2
Central(config-if)# ipv6 address 2001:db8:62::f14b:65a1/64
Central(config-if)# exit
Central(config)#
```

For interfaces exposed to possible external attack, such as the Internet interface of a border router, shut down the interface until IPv6 configuration is complete.

If the router is responsible for imposing filtering rules on IPv6 traffic, then create and apply IPv6 access lists at this step, before enabling IPv6 forwarding (see Section 3.3).

For each interface, decide whether the router should provide router advertisements and support IPv6 stateless autoconfiguration on that link. Once you have made the decision for each interface, perform the following steps:

1. For interfaces that will not provide router advertisements, disable them using the IPv6 neighbor discovery configuration command `ipv6 nd`. In our example network, the facility LAN does not need router advertisement services; they can be disabled as shown below.

    ```
    Central(config)# interface fast0/0
    Central(config-if)# ipv6 nd ra suppress
    Central(config-if)# exit
    ```

    (On older IOS releases, use `ipv6 nd suppress-ra` instead.)

2. For interfaces that will provide router advertisements and support autoconfiguration, set IPv6 neighbor discovery and autoconfiguration operational parameters using the `ipv6 nd` command. In our example network, Central will provide autoconfiguration support for LAN 2, which is 2001:db8:62::/64. The service can be configured as follows.

    ```
    Central(config)# interface fast0/1
    Central(config-if)# ipv6 nd prefix 2001:db8:62::/64
    Central(config-if)# exit
    ```

IPv6 routers have the ability to send ICMP redirects if they receive packets for forwarding that the sender should have sent differently. Disable redirects for external links and point-to-point links. To disable redirects, use the interface configuration command shown below.

```
Central(config)# interface fast0/0
Central(config-if)# no ipv6 redirects
Central(config-if)# exit
```

By default, IOS may send ICMPv6 Unreachable messages when it cannot route an incoming packet or when the packet is rejected by traffic filtering. Some IOS releases offer a command to suppress these messages. Unreachables should be suppressed on border routers' outward facing interfaces, when possible, to prevent network probing.

```
North(config)# interface eth0
North(config-if)# no ipv6 unreachables
North(config-if)# exit
```

In addition to configuring the physical interfaces and/or subinterfaces that will support IPv6, you should also configure the loopback interface. Most network services initiated by the router (e.g. outgoing Telnet connections) should use the loopback interface as their source. See section 4.1.4 of the RSCG for a discussion of the loopback interface and motivations for using it.

The loopback interface's IPv6 address should have a prefix length of 128. Note that the loopback's address cannot overlap with any other network configured on the router. The example below shows how to configure the loopback using P2.

```
Central(config)# interface loopback0
Central(config-if)# description Loopback virtual interface
Central(config-if)# ipv6 address 2001:db8:6f::ee15:f00d/128
Central(config-if)# exit
Central(config)#
```

3.2.3. Initial Setup Part 3: Enable IPv6

Finally, initiate IPv6 traffic forwarding on the router. Use the command `ipv6 unicast-routing` to begin forwarding IPv6 packets. Also, enable Cisco Express Forwarding (CEF) if the router supports it.

```
Central(config)# ipv6 unicast-routing
Central(config)# ip cef
Central(config)# ipv6 cef
Central(config)# exit
Central#
```

At this point, the router will be providing IPv6 routing services for all interfaces on which IPv6 is configured.

Verifying Initial IPv6 Configuration

After setting up all the interfaces and enabling IPv6, check your work using the `show ipv6 interface` command.

```
Central# show ipv6 interface brief
FastEthernet0/0                [up/up]
    FE80::205:32FF:FE46:5A10
    2001:db8:60::f14b:65a1
FastEthernet0/1                [up/up]
    FE80::205:32FF:FE46:5A11
    2001:db8:62::f14b:65a1
Ethernet1/2                    [administratively down/down]
    unassigned
Ethernet1/3                    [administratively down/down]
    unassigned
Loopback0                      [up/up]
    FE80::205:32FF:FE46:5A01
    2001:db8:6f::ee15:f00d
Central#
```

3.2.4. Summary of Recommendations for Initial Configuration

It is not difficult to configure IPv6 on Cisco IOS. To avoid needless security exposure, follow these principles:

- Restrict access to remote administrative services before enabling IPv6.

- Configure IPv6 addresses only on interfaces that have an operational need to support IPv6 traffic.

- Suppress router advertisements on IPv6 interfaces that will not support hosts (e.g. backbone links) or where the router is not responsible for acting as a default gateway.

3.2.5. Adding Static IPv6 Routes

In addition to setting up interfaces and addresses, your initial IPv6 configuration may require one or more static routes. These are explicit statements of IPv6 network reachability, configured on a router to help it forward traffic. The syntax for setting an IPv6 static route is shown below.

```
ipv6 route destination next-hop [ admin-distance ]
```

The destination field is an IPv6 network with mask, and the next-hop is usually an IPv6 address. The administrative distance may be supplied to make static routes less preferred than certain dynamic routes; usually it can be omitted, and static routes take precedence over dynamic routes.

The example below shows adding three static routes on router Central, a default route through North, and two /64 routes to reach LAN 3 and LAN 4 through South.

```
Central(config)# ipv6 route ::/0 2001:db8:60::e135:6ba4
Central(config)# ipv6 route 2001:db8:63::/64 2001:db8:62::43d1:805
Central(config)# ipv6 route 2001:db8:64::/64 2001:db8:62::43d1:805
```

For additional detail about any of the commands used in this section, consult the IOS *IPv6 Command Reference* [44].

3.3. IPv6 Access Lists and Packet Filtering

IOS 12.3 and later support a variety of IPv6 capabilities using access lists (ACLs): packet filtering, route mapping, service access control, rate limiting, and traffic shaping. IPv6 ACLs and IPv4 ACLs are independent; they must be defined and applied separately. Each IPv6 ACL must have a unique name, numbered ACLs are not supported for IPv6.

3.3.1. Access List Structure and Syntax

An ACL consists of a sequence of rules, each of which specifies three things:

- whether to permit (accept) or deny (reject) the packet,

- conditions that matching packets must satisfy, and

- optional additional actions to perform in response to a matching packet (such as logging a message).

The match conditions can include source and destination address matching, IPv6 header flow label and TOS field matching, the payload protocol, source and destination port matching for UDP and TCP, and message type codes for ICMP. The order of the rules in an ACL is very important: a packet will be processed according to the first rule whose conditions it satisfies.

The general syntax for defining an IPv6 access list is shown below.

```
ipv6 access-list acl-name
    rule1
    rule2
      .
      .
    exit
```

The syntax for rules is fairly complex, and different fields are allowed depending on the protocol type. The general structure is shown below.

```
{permit|deny} protocol source-spec dest-spec [addl-params]
```

For the *protocol* field, a rule can contain an explicit IPv6 next header number, or a protocol name from the list below.

ACL protocol name	IPv6 Next Header Value	Description
tcp	6	TCP – access list rules can also specify source port, and destination port, and flags.
udp	17	UDP – rules can also specify source port and destination port.
ahp	51	IPSec authentication header (AH)
esp	50	IPSec encapsulated security payload (ESP)

ACL protocol name	IPv6 Next Header Value	Description
icmp	58	ICMPv6 – rules can match message type & code.
sctp	132	Stream Control Transmission Protocol – rules can also specify source and destination ports.
ipv6	*n.a.*	Match all IPv6 packets.

The *source-spec* matching condition applies to the source address and source port of a packet. The address portion can be the keyword **any**, a single host address, or an address with prefix length. For the protocols TCP, UDP, and SCTP it may also include a source port number or range of source port numbers. Similarly, the *dest-spec* matching condition applies to the IPv6 destination address and destination port. The syntax is shown below.

{**any** | **host** *addr* | *addr/length* } [*operator portnum*]

Some operators include **eq**, **gt**, **lt**, **neq**, and **range**. Port number matching in IPv6 access list rules works exactly like that for IPv4 access list rules. Service names of many protocols may be used instead of port numbers (e.g. smtp for 25, www for 80).

Finally, the *addl-params* part of a rule can include further match conditions about the packet and additional actions for IOS to take when a packet matches the rule. The table below lists some of the additional parameters that may appear in a rule. For more detailed information, consult the IPv6 command reference [44].

ACL Keyword and Syntax	Description
dest-option-type *type* *	Matches when an option with the given type number appears in an IPv6 destination options extension header (*type*=1..255).
dscp *value*	Matches when the IPv6 header traffic class field contains a particular differentiated services code point (DSCP) *value*.
established	Matches TCP packets that are part of an established connection. Applies to TCP only.
flow-label *value*	Matches IPv6 packets where the header contains a flow label equal to *value*.
fragments	Matches non-initial fragments. May not be used in the same rule with port numbers.
log	Instructs IOS to log a message when a packet matches the rule.
log-input	Instructs IOS to log a message, including the name of the input interface, when a packet matches the rule.
mobility *	Matches when the packet includes a mobility header. (Part of Mobile IPv6, see Section 5.2.)

ACL Keyword and Syntax	Description
`reflect` `acl-name` `*`	Instructs IOS to modify the ACL *acl-name* to allow return traffic corresponding to the matching packet (this is part of IOS's reflexive access list feature)
`routing` `*`	Matches when a packet includes a routing header.
`routing-type` `type` `*`	Matches when a packet includes a routing header of the specified routing *type*.
TCP flag: `fin|rst|syn|urg`	Matches when the packet is a TCP packet and the specified flag bit is set. TCP only.
ICMP: `type` `[code]` `|` `message`	Matches ICMPv6 packets that contain the particular *type* and *code* values. IOS allows symbolic message names for common messages. Some of the names are: `echo-request`, `echo-reply`, `nd-na`, `nd-ns`, `no-route`, and `packet-too-big`.
`sequence` `number`	Determines the location in the access list to add the rule. By default, each new rule you add gets appended to the access list. Using the sequence parameter, you can insert rules precisely at the desired point in an access list without re-creating the entire list.
`time-range` `name`	Matches only when the current time of day falls within the specified time range *name*. Usable only with permit rules. Create named time ranges using the command `time-range`.
`undetermined-transport` `*`	Matches packets where the transport-layer protocol is unknown or cannot be determined. Usable only with deny rules.

IPv6 access list rules are complex, but they offer you rich functionality for selectively processing and forwarding traffic. The parameters marked with an asterisk (*) are not available in some earlier versions of IOS or on some Cisco platforms.

IPv6 access lists can also contain comments, using the keyword `remark`. Use comments to document the intent and organization of your access lists. Access list entries can have sequence numbers, which can help with maintenance (see page 43).

In addition to the rules you define for an access list, every IPv6 access list applied to an interface gets three implicit rules at the end: two permitting neighbor discovery, and the third denying all other packets. In other words, every IPv6 traffic filter has the following 'invisible' rules at the end:

```
permit icmp any any nd-na
permit icmp any any nd-ns
deny ipv6 any any
```

The two permit rules match neighbor advertisements and neighbor solicition messages, respectively; the deny statement matches all IPv6 packets. The two permit rules allow the message types that are essential for correct operation of neighbor discovery and related control procedures. You can override these implicit rules with explicit rules of yours, but do it carefully to avoid blocking neighbor discovery.

3.3.2. Using Access Lists to Filter IPv6 Traffic

IOS supports IPv6 traffic filtering on all IPv6 network interfaces, including virtual interfaces such as tunnels. You can apply one filter for outgoing packets, and one filter for incoming packets. The two filters are independent (unless you employ advanced features like reflexive access lists or the IOS Firewall). Figure 14 illustrates this concept.

In the figure, packets from network A must pass the inbound filter on interface eth0 before it will be processed or forwarded by the router. Similarly, packets to be sent over network A must pass the outbound filter on eth0. A packet sent from a host on network A to host on network B will have to pass the inbound filter on eth0 and the outbound filter on eth1.

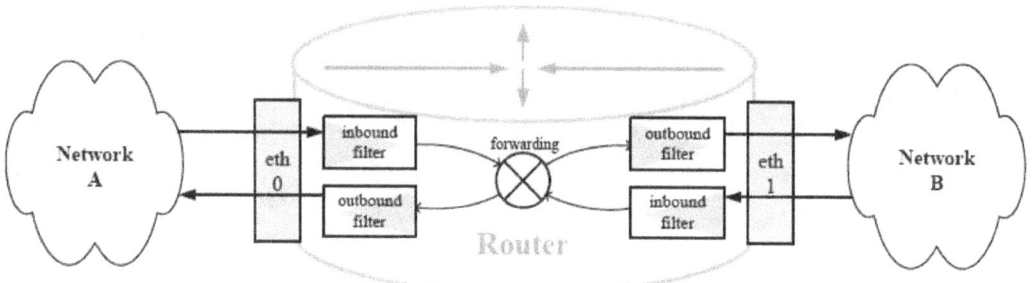

Figure 14: IPv6 Traffic Filters

To use an access list as a traffic filter on an interface, enter interface configuration mode and use the command below.

```
ipv6 traffic-filter acl-name {in | out}
```

With the keyword **in**, the access list will be applied to all IPv6 packets received on the interface, and with keyword **out**, all IPv6 packets about to be transmitted on the interface. Keep the following points in mind when configuring traffic filters.

- IOS will not report an error if the access list named for an interface traffic filter does not exist. (This is not a bug. It allows you to set the filter first and then define the access list later.) To avoid potential problems, check your spelling carefully.

- An outbound filter will not block packets generated by the router itself. (For example, an outbound ACL that blocks ICMPv6 echo-request messages will not drop echo-request messages generated by a **ping** command executed on the router, but it will drop those being forwarded through the router.)

- Traffic filters on interfaces do not directly influence how IOS routes traffic. Forwarding decisions are made before traffic filters are applied.

3.3.3. Access List Examples

This sub-section shows two example access lists, merely to illustrate IPv6 access list syntax and construction. Use these examples to learn the syntax of IPv6 ACLs.

Example 1

The first example shows a simple access list permitting all traffic from LAN 3 and LAN 4, and permitting only TCP port 80 traffic from the remote LAN. (Note: use the 'no' form of the command first, to remove any prior definition of the access-list.)

```
East# config t
Enter configuration commands, one per line. End with CNTL/Z
East(config)# no ipv6 access-list ex1-admin-inbound
East(config)# ipv6 access-list ex1-admin-inbound
East(config-ipv6-acl)# remark allow traffic from LAN 3 and 4
East(config-ipv6-acl)# permit ipv6 2001:db8:63::/64 any
East(config-ipv6-acl)# permit ipv6 2001:db8:64::/64 any
East(config-ipv6-acl)# remark allow only www from Remote LAN
East(config-ipv6-acl)# permit tcp 2001:db8:20::/64 any eq 80
East(config-ipv6-acl)# exit
East(config)#
```

This access list could be used to restrict the traffic destined for the Admin LAN and the router East. To apply an IPv6 access list to a network interface, use the command `ipv6 traffic-filter` in interface configuration mode.

```
East(config)# interface eth0
East(config-if)# description Facility LAN interface
East(config-if)# ipv6 traffic-filter ex1-admin-inbound in
East(config-if)# exit
East(config)#
```

To remove the traffic filter from an interface, use the `no ipv6 traffic-filter` command, as shown below.

```
East(config)# interface eth0
East(config-if)# no ipv6 traffic-filter in
East(config-if)# exit
East#
```

Example 2

The second example shows a more complicated access list. This access list includes the following rules, to illustrate some additional access list features.

- Deny all traffic to the deprecated site-local address range, and log all violations.

- Deny packets with an unknown or invalid payload protocol, and log all violations.

- Deny traffic to non-link-local multicast addresses.

- Deny packets that include a routing header, and log violations.

- Permit TCP traffic to web servers (ports 80 and 443).

- Permit TCP and UDP traffic to DNS servers (port 53).

- Permit TCP traffic on the SMTP port only from the mail server, 2001:db8:60::45.

- Permit ESP traffic only to a specific address on the Remote LAN, 2001:db8:20::150.

- Deny ICMPv6 echo-reply messages, and log all violations, but permit all other ICMPv6.

When a packet is undergoing processing against an access list, the first rule that applies to the packet determines its fate. IOS does not attempt to find a 'best' match, but simply uses the first one. Therefore, the order of rules in your access lists are very important.

```
Central(config)# ipv6 access-list ex2-outbound
Central(config-ipv6-acl)# remark prohibit use of site-local
Central(config-ipv6-acl)# deny ipv6 fec0::/10  any    log-input
Central(config-ipv6-acl)# deny ipv6 any fec0::/10   log-input
Central(config-ipv6-acl)# remark prohibit unknown protocols
Central(config-ipv6-acl)# deny ipv6 any any undetermined-trans
Central(config-ipv6-acl)# remark allow only link-local multicst
Central(config-ipv6-acl)# permit ipv6 any ff02::/16
Central(config-ipv6-acl)# deny ipv6 any ff00::/8
Central(config-ipv6-acl)# remark prohibit IPv6 routing header
Central(config-ipv6-acl)# deny ipv6 any any routing  log-input
Central(config-ipv6-acl)# remark allow HTTP and DNS requests
Central(config-ipv6-acl)# permit tcp any any eq 80
Central(config-ipv6-acl)# permit tcp any any eq 443
Central(config-ipv6-acl)# permit tcp any any eq 53
Central(config-ipv6-acl)# permit udp any any eq 53
Central(config-ipv6-acl)# remark allow SMTP from mail server
Central(config-ipv6-acl)# permit tcp host 2001:db8:60::45
                                       any eq 25
Central(config-ipv6-acl)# remark allow ESP only to remote VPN
Central(config-ipv6-acl)# permit esp any host 2001:db8:20::150
Central(config-ipv6-acl)# remark prohibit ping responses
Central(config-ipv6-acl)# deny icmp any any echo-reply log-input
Central(config-ipv6-acl)# remark allow all other ICMP
Central(config-ipv6-acl)# permit icmp any any
Central(config-ipv6-acl)# exit
Central(config)# exit
```

After you create or modify an access list, always review it for accuracy. Use the command **show ipv6 access-list** *name* to display the access list. Note that remarks will appear in the IOS configuration listing, but not in the access-list display.

```
Central# show ipv6 access-list ex2-outbound
IPv6 access list ex2-outbound
    deny ipv6 FEC0::/10 any log-input sequence 10
    deny ipv6 any FEC0::/10 log-input sequence 20
    deny ipv6 any any undetermined-transport sequence 50
    permit ipv6 any FF02::/16 sequence 70
    deny ipv6 any FF00::/8 log-input sequence 80
    deny ipv6 any any log-input routing sequence 100
    permit tcp any any eq www sequence 120
    permit tcp any any eq 443 sequence 130
    permit tcp any any eq domain sequence 140
    permit udp any any eq domain sequence 150
    permit tcp host 2001:DB8:60::45 any eq smtp sequence 170
    permit esp any host 2001:DB8:20::150 sequence 190
    deny icmp any any echo-reply log-input sequence 210
    permit icmp any any sequence 230
Central#
```

The transcript below shows how to apply this filter to outbound traffic on the Central router's interface fast0/0.

```
Central(config)# interface fast0/0
Central(config-if)# description Facility LAN interface
Central(config-if)# ipv6 traffic-filter ex2-outbound out
Central(config-if)# exit
```

After you apply an access list to an interface, you can check it using the command **show ipv6 interface**. More information about checking IPv6 configuration, and example commands, appear in Section 3.4.

3.3.4. Maintaining IPv6 Named Access Lists

Note that, while sequence numbers allow you to insert rules into an access list without rebuilding the list, it is not a good practice to revise or rewrite operational access-lists on-the-fly. A better practice is to keep operational traffic filters stored off-line, under configuration management, and update entire access lists by uploading them or pasting them from the managed, off-line copy.

To avoid potential problems and windows of exposure during access list updates, each update to a critical access list should be given a unique name. One good approach is to name the access list with a date and sequence number.

A file holding the example 2 access list updated on 22 Nov 2005 would look something like this:

```
ipv6 access-list ex2-outbound-20051122-01
 remark prohibit use of site-local
 deny ipv6 fec0::/10    any    log-input
   .
   .
     .
 permit icmp any any
 exit
```

When modifying or revising the access list, edit the file, and update the access list name. After a revision on Nov 28, 2005, the file would look like this:

```
ipv6 access-list ex2-outbound-20051128-01
 remark prohibit ICMP to multicast addresses
 deny icmp any ff00::/8 log
 remark prohibit use of site-local
 deny ipv6 fec0::/10    any    log-input
     .
     .
 permit icmp any any
 exit
```

To update the access list, perform the following steps in order:

1. Upload the new access list into the running configuration using the **copy** command with FTP or (preferably) SCP. If the new access list has any syntax errors, messages will appear during this step; do not continue, but fix the errors and then start at step 1 again.

2. Check that the new access list uploaded correctly, using the **show ipv6 access-list** command.

3. Apply the new access list to the intended interface(s) using the **ipv6 traffic-filter** command.

4. Check that the new access list is installed and working as intended (checking functionality usually must be done from some other host, not the router).

5. Delete the old access list, if necessary.

Note that the new access list will have fresh match counters.

The transcript below shows an update using the recommend procedure.

```
Central# copy scp://bsjones@[2001:db8:62::3f6]/acls/ex2-
outbound.acl.txt running-config
Destination filename[running-config]:  return
Password: password
!
567 bytes copied in 5.27 seconds
Central# show ipv6 access-list ex2-out-20051128-02
IPv6 access list ex2-out-20051128-02
    deny ipv6 FEC0::/10 any log-input sequence 10
    deny ipv6 any FEC0::/10 log-input sequence 20
        .
        .

    permit icmp any any sequence 140
Central# config t
Enter configuration commands, one per line. End with CNTL/Z
Central(config)# interface fast0/0
```

```
Central(config-if)# ipv6 traffic-filter ex2-out-20051128-02 out
Central(config-if)# exit
Central(config)# exit
Central# show ipv6 interface fast0/0
FastEthernet0/0 is up, line protocol is up
  IPv6 is enabled, link-local address FE80::20C:85FF:FE5A:AD91
  Global unicast address(es):
    2001:db8:60::f14b:65a1, subnet is 2001:db8:60:/64
    .
    .
  Output features: ACL
  Outgoing access list ex2-out-20051128-02
    .
    .
Central# config t
Enter configuration commands, one per line. End with CNTL/Z
Central(config)# no ipv6 access-list ex2-out-20051128-01
Central(config)# exit
Central#
```

3.3.5. Recommended Border Router Filtering

This sub-section describes design objectives for IPv6 traffic filtering at the boundary between an IPv6 enclave network and the rest of a large internet (or the Internet).

For incoming traffic, an enclave should enforce some version of these IPv6 rules at its border. Additional rules may be warranted for a particular site.

Recommendations

In general, it is best to craft rules that permit necessary traffic and then reject all other traffic. The 'first-match' processing model for IPv6 access lists makes it necessary, in many cases, to use a mixture of deny and permit rules in your access lists. Tables 1 and 2, below, give general recommendations for filtering. Following them, two example access lists show how to implement the recommendations on IOS.

Filter Table 1: General Recommendations for Filtering Inbound Traffic

The goal for filtering inbound packets is to accept only those packets that have a legitimate reason for entering the enclave network or the router itself. Rules in bold have no conditions and should be applied for all network boundaries, the other rules may be applied selectively, depending on your network configuration and service profile.

Inbound Traffic Rule	Rationale
reject multicast source addresses	Illegal address – multicast source addresses are prohibited by the IPv6 standards.
reject site-local source or destination addresses	Bad address – the site local addresses are officially deprecated.

Inbound Traffic Rule	Rationale
reject internal source addresses	Bad address – incoming packets should never have internal source addresses.
reject IPv4 compatibility source or destination addresses	Bad address – these addresses should never appear as source or destination addresses in normal IPv6 traffic.
reject destination addresses in the 6to4 reserved address range (2002::/16), if your site is not supporting 6to4 services and is not providing transit service	Reserved address – addresses in the 6to4 range should only be allowed when the site is explicitly hosting 6to4 routers or relay routers.
reject all packets with routing headers if internal network is not supporting home agents or hosting mobile hosts, otherwise reject only packets with type 0 routing headers	Reserved header – type 2 routing headers should only appear when hosting mobile hosts or running a home agent for Mobile IPv6. Type 0 routing headers should always be blocked at enclave boundaries.
reject traffic with source or destination addresses in the unique local range (fc00::/16) at the enterprise boundary	Reserved address – addresses in the unique local range are for use within local scopes only, they should not appear on the Internet.
allow destination addresses of internal networks only, unless your network provides transit services (also, allow destinations in global multicast range)	Probing defense – a router's normal response to bad addresses is to send an ICMPv6 error; by dropping the packets with an ACL, you deprive the attacker of valuable information.
allow only specific, necessary protocols [probably TCP, UDP, ICMPv6, and ESP, but possibly others like OSPF or PIM]	Generally, it is better to write rules that permit specific protocols rather than reject all the many others.
allow only specific, necessary ICMPv6 messages types	probing defense – only permit ICMPv6 messages required for correct and efficient operation of IPv6.
allow only necessary destination port ranges; if the site is not providing any externally accessible services, then block registered port range, otherwise limit registered port range to specific server destination addresses	probing and scanning defense – deprive attackers of the ability to perform port scans and attempt accesses to non-public network services.
allow tunneling only to specific, identified hosts that are authorized to host tunnels (e.g. mobile IPv6 home agents)	illicit traffic defense – tunnels can be used for inappropriate and malicious traffic; only permit tunnel traffic to designated, authorized tunnel servers.

Filter Table 2: General Recommendations for Filtering Outbound Traffic

The goal for filtering outbound packets is to allow packets to leave the internal network when they appear valid and authorized. What constitutes authorized traffic will vary considerably, depending on your network architecture, types of firewalls and servers installed on the network, and strictness of enclave security policies.

Outbound Traffic Rule	Rationale
reject multicast source addresses	illegal address – multicast source addresses are prohibited by the IPv6 standards.
reject site-local source or destination addresses	bad address – the site-local addresses are official deprecated.
reject IPv4 compatibility source or destination addresses	bad address – these addresses should not appear as source or destination addresses in normal IPv6 traffic.
reject mobility extension header if internal network is not acting as a home agent or hosting mobile hosts	reserved header – should only appear when hosting mobile hosts or running a home agent for Mobile IPv6. (Some releases do not suppport matching on this header.)
reject type 0 routing header (unless source routing is needed – unlikely)	Reserved header – type 1 routing headers are used only for source routing.
reject unique local addresses at enterprise boundaries	Internal-use addresses – unique local addresses are for internal enterprise use only, they should not be routed on the Internet.
allow only valid destination addresses (i.e. for the Internet, allocated IPv6 ranges: 2001::16, 2002::/16, and 3ffe::/16, or just simply 2000::/3, and global scope multicast)	bogon defense – hosts on your network should not be injecting improper traffic onto the global Internet.
allow only valid internal source addresses (unless your network provides transit services)	Bad address – only compromised hosts will be sending traffic with bogus source addresses, all such traffic should be blocked.
allow only specific, necessary protocols [probably TCP, UDP, ICMPv6, and ESP, but possibly others like OSPF or SCTP]	Generally, it is better to write rules that permit specific protocols rather than reject all the many others.
allow only specific, necessary ICMPv6 messages types	Probing defense – only permit ICMPv6 messages required for correct and efficient operation of IPv6.
allow only necessary source port ranges; if the site is not providing any externally accessible services, then block registered port range, otherwise limit registered ports to specific server destination addresses	Probing and scanning defense – deprive attackers of the ability to perform port scans and attempt accesses to non-public network services.
allow tunneling only from specific, identified hosts that are authorized to host tunnels (e.g. mobile IPv6 home agents)	Illicit traffic defense – tunnels can be used for inappropriate and malicious traffic; only permit tunnel traffic to designated, authorized tunnel servers.

Filter Table 3: ICMPv6 Message Types

There are many ICMPv6 message types necessary for the correct operation of IPv6. The table below lists relevant messages types, and whether they should be allowed inbound or outbound from a protected enclave. (In general, allow only ICMPv6 messages that are necessary for the operation of your network, and block all others.)

ICMPv6 Message Type	Allow In?	Allow Out?	Remarks
Destination unreachable (1)	Y	n	This message type is very useful for probing and network mapping; allow only to trusted partners.
Packet-too-big (2)	Y	Y	Allow this, it is necessary for PMTUD.
Time exceeded (3)	Y	n	While this message is necessary, in theory, for correct operation of IPv6, in practice it only facilitates probing.
Parameter problem (4)	Y	n?	May not wish to allow this message type out of the network; it can be used for probing.
Echo request (128)	n	Y	Allow echo requests outbound if you want to allow internal hosts to ping external hosts. Consider allowing echo requests to the router.
Echo reply (129)	Y	n	Prohibit echo reply outbound.
MLD (130-132)	n	Y	These messages are needed within your network, but not on external router-to-router links. If the external network segment does not support hosts, then block MLD reports (type 131) inbound.
ND (135-136)	Y	Y	Allow these link-local messages, they are necessary for correct operation of IPv6.
RD (133-134)	Y?	Y	If the external network segment does not support hosts, then block these messages inbound.
Redirect (135)	Y?	Y	Depending on the type of external network segment, this message can be necessary for correct operations; allow them inbound unless the external link connects exactly two routers.
Node information (139-140)	n	n	The node information query and response messages are not widely implemented, but can be used for probing. Prohibit them.
Inverse ND (141-142)	n	n	These messages are not widely implemented, but can be used for probing.
Mobility support (144-147)	n?	n?	These messages are defined in RFC 3775 [36], and are used by mobile nodes and home agents. If your network supports a home agent or allows mobile nodes, then allow these ICMP message types, otherwise prohibit them.

Example Access Lists

The examples access lists below show border router filtering for the router North. (Lines that are too wide for the page are shown wrapped with a backslash

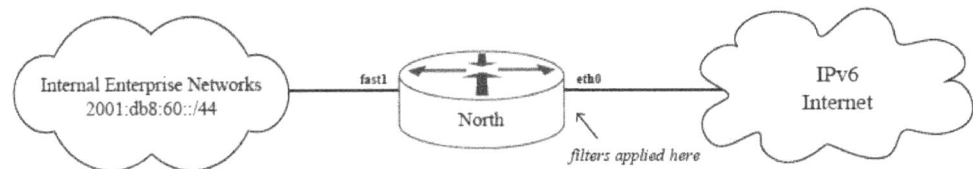

Figure 15: Context for Border Router Filtering Examples

The example inbound filter access list is shown below. Each section is labeled.

```
ipv6 access-list border-inbound-ex
  remark reject multicast source addresses
  deny ipv6 ff00::/16            any                    log
  remark reject site-local and ipv4-compatibility addresses
  deny ipv6 fc00::/10            any                    log
  deny ipv6 any                  fc00::/10              log
  deny ipv6 0::/96               any                    log
  deny ipv6 any                  0::/96                 log
  remark reject 6to4 destination (if not providing 6to4 relays)
  deny ipv6 any                  2002::/16              log
  remark reject external traffic with internal source addr
  deny ipv6 2001:db8:60::/44     any                    log
  remark reject unique local, should be confined our network
  deny ipv6 any                  fc00::/16              log
  deny ipv6 fc00::/16            any                    log
  remark reject type 0 routing header
  deny ipv6 any                  any  routing-type 0 log
  remark allow incoming TCP connections to specific servers
  permit tcp any    host 2001:db8:60::80  eq www
  permit tcp any    host 2001:db8:60::80 eq 443
  permit tcp any    host 2001:db8:60::25 eq smtp
  remark allow BGP sessions either way for external BGP peer
  permit tcp    host 2001:db8:2::1 host 2001:db8:2::2 eq bgp
  permit tcp    host 2001:db8:2::1 eq bgp host 2001:db8:2::2
  remark allow incoming TCP on non-reserved ports
  permit tcp any    2001:db8:60::/44     range 1024 65535
  remark allow DNS requests to the public DNS server
  permit udp any    host 2001:db8:60::53 eq domain
  remark allow responses to outgoing DNS back to any host
  permit udp any eq domain  2001:db8:60::/44
  remark allow IPSec and IKE between North and Remote
  permit udp    host 2001:db8:2f::2 eq 500 \
        host 2001:db8:6f::2 eq 500
  permit esp    host 2001:db8:2f::2   host 2001:db8:6f::2
  remark allow UDP to non-reserved ports with destination \
        of our net or global multicast
  permit udp  any  2001:db8:60::/44    gt 1023
  permit udp  any  ffe0::/12           gt 1023
  remark allow specific ICMP types inbound to global addresses
  permit icmp any  2001:db8:60::/44    destination-unreachable
  permit icmp any  2001:db8:60::/44    packet-too-big
  permit icmp any  2001:db8:60::/44    parameter-problem
  permit icmp any  2001:db8:60::/44    echo-reply
  remark allow ping from our partners at remote site
```

```
    permit icmp 2001:db8:20::/44   2001:db8:60::/44  echo-request
    remark allow ND and MLD ICMP types generally, but not RD
    permit icmp any   any              nd-na
    permit icmp any   any              nd-ns
    permit icmp any   any              mld-query
    permit icmp any   any              mld-reduction
    remark allow tunnel traffic only to North and Central routers
    permit 41   any   host 2001:db8:6f::2
    permit 41   any   host 2001:db8:60::f14b:65a1
    remark reject everything else
    deny    ipv6 any any log
```

The example outbound access list for router North is shown below.

```
ipv6 access-list border-outbound-ex
  remark reject multicast source addresses
  deny ipv6 ff00::/16              any                  log
  remark reject site-local and ipv4-compatibility addresses
  deny ipv6 fc00::/10              any                  log
  deny ipv6 any                    fc00::/10            log
  deny ipv6 0::/96                 any                  log
  deny ipv6 any                    0::/96               log
  remark reject unique local, should not exit our network
  deny ipv6 any                    fc00::/16            log
  deny ipv6 fc00::/16              any                  log
  remark reject type 0 routing header
  deny ipv6 any                 any routing-type 0  log
  remark allow outbound TCP from specific servers
  permit tcp host 2001:db8:60::80  eq www   2000::/3
  permit tcp host 2001:db8:60::80  eq 443   2000::/3
  permit tcp host 2001:db8:60::25  eq smtp  2000::/3
  remark allow outbound TCP from non-reserved ports
  permit tcp    2001:db8:60::/44 gt 1023      2000::/3
  remark allow BGP sessions either way for our BGP peer
  permit tcp    host 2001:db8:6f::2 eq bgp host 2001:db8:6f::1
  permit tcp    host 2001:db8:6f::2 host 2001:db8:6f::1 eq bgp
  remark allow UDP to valid addresses and global multicast
  permit udp    2001:db8:60::/44    2000::/3
  permit udp    2001:db8:60::/44    ffe0::/12
  remark allow specific ICMP messages out to everywhere
  permit icmp   2001:db8:60::/44    2000::/3  packet-too-big
  permit icmp   2001:db8:60::/44    2000::/3  parameter-problem
  permit icmp   2001:db8:60::/44    2000::/3  echo-request
  remark allow some ICMP just to our partners at remote site
  permit icmp   2001:db8:60::/44    2001:db8:20::/44  \
                            destination-unreachable
  permit icmp   2001:db8:60::/44 2001:db8:20::/44 echo-reply
  remark allow tunnels only from North and Central routers
  permit 41      host 2001:db8:6f::2           any
  permit 41      host 2001:db8:60::f14b:65a1  any
  remark deny everything else
  deny ipv6 any any log
```

Installing these two access lists on North's Internet-facing interface is very easy.

```
North(config)# interface eth0
North(config-if)# ipv6 traffic-filter border-inbound-ex in
North(config-if)# ipv6 traffic-filter border-outbound-ex out
North(config-if)# exit
North(config)#
```

Note that the ACLs above are just examples. While they illustrate the syntax and a usable approach, they would need to be tailored and customized to your specific network needs before putting them on an operational border router.

Finally, note that a filtering router is not usually a sufficient safeguard, by itself, to enforce security policy at enclave boundaries. In most cases, firewall functionality is also needed. With the right feature set, an IOS router can serve as a simple firewall (see Section 4.3), and many commercial firewall appliances now support IPv6.

3.4. IPv6 Reverse-Path Verification, Rate Limiting, and Control-Plane Policing

Rate limiting and Unicast Reverse-Path Forwarding (uRPF) verification are important security mechanisms that can help defend your networks in the router's data plane. By using rate limiting, you can control the amount of bandwidth consumed by different kinds of traffic, different subnets, or different protocols. URPF is a powerful capability for rejecting traffic with fake or spoofed source addresses; it can help defend your network from malicious traffic and also help prevent your network from being used as a source of malicious traffic sent to others.

3.4.1. Using Unicast Reverse-Path Forwarding Verification

This subsection describes uRPF, and shows how to use it to verify IPv6 traffic. For more details, consult [41] and [49].

What Is uRPF?

Internally, IOS stores very detailed routing information in the form of a Forwarding Information Base (FIB). When Cisco Express Forwarding (CEF) is enabled, the FIB contains enough information to verify that a packet arriving on an interface *should* be arriving there. The test works by performing a reverse lookup into the FIB: a packet from address X arriving on interface Y is deemed valid only if interface Y would be the best way to send a packet back to X. Because it uses the same data structures built for routing, uRPF verification is very fast and automatic. Most IOS releases 12.3 and later that support IPv6 also support uRPF for IPv6.

Figure 16 illustrates the concepts behind uRPF. In the figure, uRPF is enabled on interface fast0/1, and two packets have been received on that interface. Each packet's source address is tested against the FIB. Packet 1, with source address 2001:db8:62::6, passes the test because the reverse-path verification shows that fast0/1 is a best path to the 2001:db8:62::/64 network. Packet 2, with bogus source address 2001:4a::1, fails because fast0/1 is not a valid path to any 2001:4a:: network.

Traffic filtering (ACLs) and uRPF may be used together, and often are. If an inbound ACL is present on an interface, then it is applied first. If the inbound ACL does not drop the packet, then it undergoes uRPF testing. If uRPF does not drop the packet, then it gets forwarded in the normal manner.

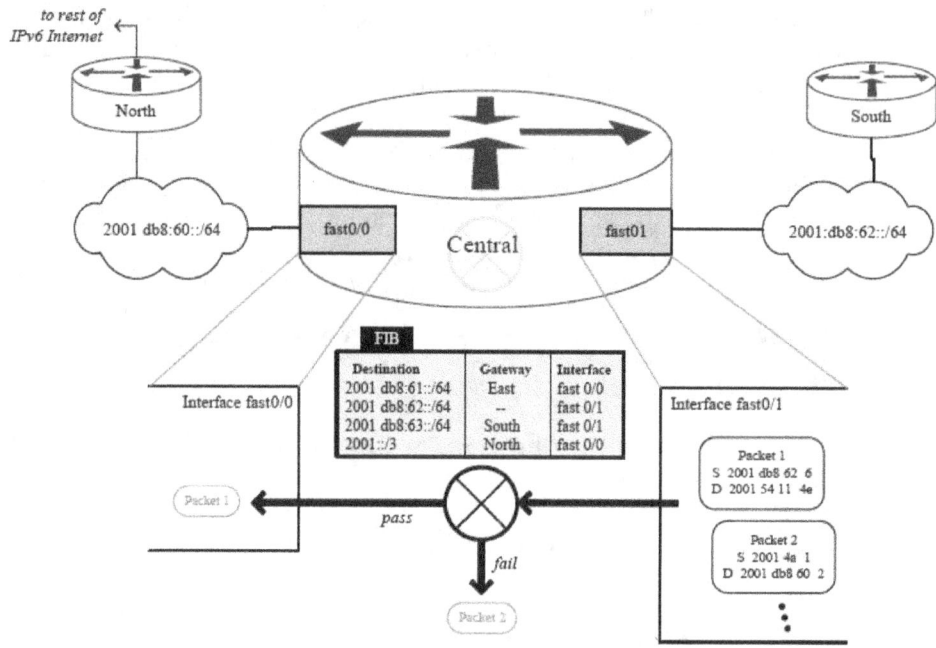

Figure 16: IPv6 Unicast Reverse-Path Forwarding Verification

There are two basic modes of uRPF: loose and strict. In strict mode, as explained above, a packet must arrive on the interface that is a best path for sending to its source address. In loose mode, the FIB must merely contain some path to the packet's source address. Strict mode is stronger and should be used where possible. When your network architecture allows asymmetric paths, so that packets may legally arrive on an interface that would not be a best reverse path, use strict mode with an ACL, or loose mode if your router supports it.

Configuring uRPF

uRPF depends on Cisco Express Forwarding. Enable CEF before configuring uRPF.

```
Central(config)# ipv6 cef
```

Select one or more interfaces on which to apply uRPF. On interfaces where there is no possibility of asymmetric paths, use strict mode. On interfaces where traffic might use asymmetric paths, use loose mode, or uRPF with an ACL, or don't enable uRPF at all. uRPF must be enabled separately on each interface, as shown below.

The table below shows syntax for uRPF interface configuration commands. Note that the first command works on a wide variety of IOS routers, but the second one appears to be supported only on higher-end models (e.g. GSR 12000).

Command Syntax	Description
`ipv6 verify unicast reverse-path [access-list]`	**Strict mode** - each incoming packet's source address tested against the FIB, if the interface is not a best reverse path, the packet fails. By default, failed packets get dropped. If an IPv6 access list is supplied, then failed packets are tested against the access list, and dropped or forwarded as specified by the access list rules.
`ipv6 verify unicast source reachable-via any [access-list]`	**Loose mode** - each incoming packet's source address is tested against the FIB, if the source is not reachable via any interface on the router, then the packet fails. If no access list is specified, failed packets are dropped, otherwise they are handled as specified by the access list rules. For details, consult [44]. (Note: available on only some IOS routers.)

The transcript below shows how to apply strict uRPF to an interface.

```
Central(config)# interface fast0/0
Central(config-if)# ipv6 verify unicast reverse-path
Central(config-if)# exit
Central(config)#
```

The general operation of uRPF is automatic for interfaces where it is enabled: every inbound packet either passes or fails. You can specify an access list to handle packets that fail the uRPF check. This is useful when you know that certain traffic will use asymmetric routes, or to force more detailed logging of uRPF events. Figure 17 shows an example network architecture where packets from a remote site can legitimately arrive over two different paths.

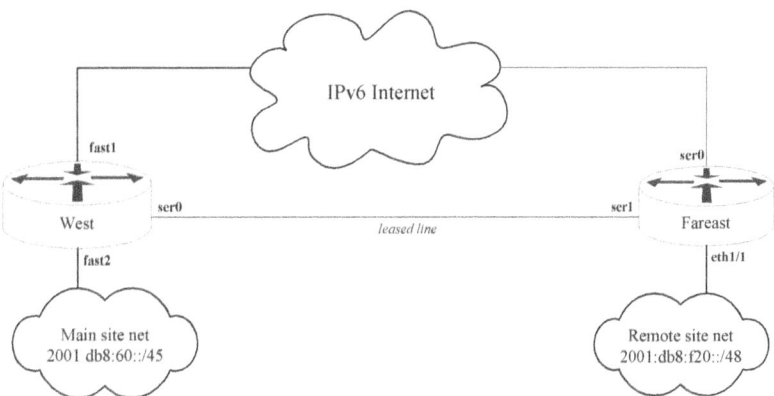

Figure 17: Network with Multiple Valid Paths

In the network shown in Figure 17, traffic between the main site net and the remote site net has two valid paths: via the Internet, or via the dedicated leased line between the sites. The leased line is the best path, but traffic that arrives over the Internet should not be dropped. Also, uRPF violations should be logged. The transcript below shows how to use uRPF with an ACL in this situation.

```
West# config t
Enter configuration commands, one per line. End with CNTL/Z
West(config)# ipv6 route 2001:db8:f20::/48 ser0
West(config)# ipv6 access-list inet-urpf-acl
West(config-ipv6-acl)# permit ipv6 2001:db8:f20::/48 any
West(config-ipv6-acl)# deny ipv6 any any log-input
West(config-ipv6-acl)# exit
West(config)# interface fast1
West(config-if)# description Internet primary ethernet
West(config-if)# ipv6 verify unicast reverse-path inet-urpf-acl
West(config-if)# end
West#
```

To disable uRPF on an interface, use `no ipv6 verify unicast reverse-path`.

Verifying uRPF

To check whether uRPF has been applied to an interface, check the IPv6 status of that interface.

```
West# show ipv6 interface fast1
FastEthernet1 is up, line protocol is up
  IPv6 is enabled, link-local address is FE80::20C:85FF:FE5B:AD91
   .
    .
  Input features: RPF
  Output features: ACL
  Unicast RPF
    Process Switching:
      0 verification drops
      0 suppressed verification drops
    CEF Switching:
      4 verification drops
   .
    .
West#
```

Setting up uRPF is easy, but troubleshooting problems with it can be tricky. To test how uRPF would handle a particular source address, use the `show ipv6 cef` command to look up the address in the FIB.

```
West# show ipv6 cef 2001:db8:f20::31 detail
2001:db8:f20::/64 RIBfib
  recursive via 2001:db8:66::54b:f629
      attached to Serial0
West#
```

The output, above, shows that uRPF will be expecting packets from the 2001:db8:f20::/64 network to arrive on interface Serial0. Packets from that address range arriving on any other interface will fail reverse-path verification.

3.4.2. Using Rate-Limiting and Control-Plane Policing

What are Rate-Limiting and Control-Plane Policing?

By default, all packets on the data plane are treated equally. A router makes its best effort at forwarding every packet, and no portion of the traffic gets preferential treatment. This impartiality may not match your network engineering or security goals. Some kinds of traffic may be more important, and others less. Some kinds of traffic may need to be throttled to keep them from consuming too much bandwidth.

A typical Cisco router performs routing and traffic forwarding using fast, dedicated hardware. Routers are designed this way to permit high throughput for traffic through the router, and rate-limiting offers you a means for regulating that traffic. Some potential uses for rate-limiting are listed below, for more information see [50].

- Reserving a portion of interface bandwidth for particular operational protocols (e.g. VoIP, chat, video) or essential control protocols (e.g. BGP).

- Limiting control protocols, such as ICMP, to only a specified small fraction of available bandwidth.

- Balancing bandwidth usage among different enterprise subnets.

- Constrain control and management plane traffic (see CPP section, below).

- Mitigate specific network attacks or worm traffic.

This section provides a very brief introduction to rate limiting and QoS policy. Cisco's web site offers technical notes, white papers, and design examples [51].

Primarily a data plane facility, rate-limiting is useful for controlling traffic through the router. It is often used commercially to support quality-of-service (QoS) requirements and service-level agreements; it can also be used to reduce threats from some kinds of attacks, and to throttle some kinds of potentially hostile traffic.

Even when rate-limiting and filtering are imposed, traffic on the data plane should flow through the router at approximately the speed of the interface links. However, the router must perform management and control functions using its own central processor (also sometimes called the "main CPU" or the "route processor"). Different router models' central processors vary in speed, but generally they cannot handle nearly as much traffic as the interface and routing hardware can. Therefore, it is possible for some denial-of-service attacks to target the router's central processor and disrupt management and control communications. Under such an attack, routing table updates may be missed, logging may be degraded, and remote administration may even become impossible. Control-plane policing (CPP) is a mechanism for rate-limiting traffic to and from the central processor; it can be used to protect the limited bandwidth between the network and the central processor.

Figure 18 shows where rate-limiting and CPP apply in a router's architecture.

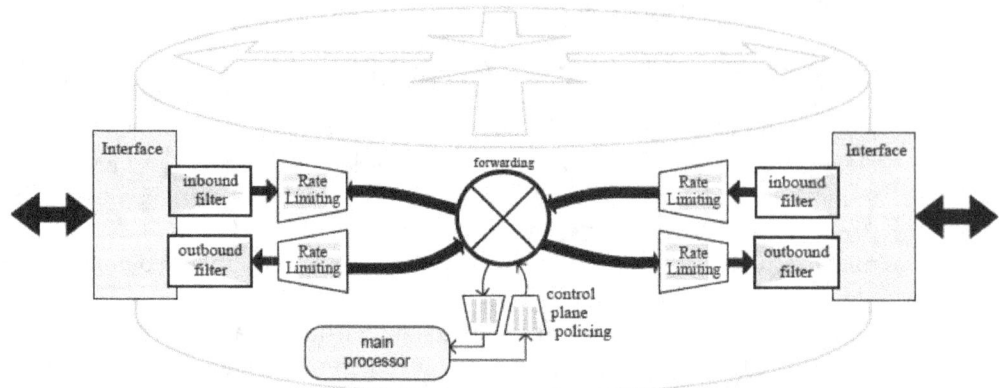

Figure 18: Conceptual View of Rate-Limiting and Control Plane Policing

Note that traffic filters are applied 'closer' to the wire than rate limiting. This is especially important for inbound filtering and rate limiting: only packets that are permitted by the inbound filter ACL count toward the bandwidth limits.

Applying Rate-Limiting to Traffic

To set up rate-limiting on traffic through your router, follow the steps listed below.

1. Design your policy goals – identify the types of traffic for which you need to reserve or restrict bandwidth, designate bandwidth reservations or ceilings, and note any special cases or exceptions. This step is essential; trying to design rate-limiting on-the-fly at the router console is counter-productive and very likely to cause service disruption.

2. Define classes – for each type of traffic listed in your policy, create a named class map. The easiest way to do this is to create an IPv6 access list for the traffic, and then define a class map based on the access list.

3. Create policies – define one or more policy maps that associates rate limits and minimum bandwidth guarantees with each class. (Typically, you'll need two maps to apply rate limiting in both directions.)

4. Apply policies – apply the policies to each interface where rate limits are needed, using the interface configuration command `service-policy`.

A class map consists of a name and one or more matching rules. Use the command `class-map match-any classname` to define a class map where matching any one of the rules gains membership in the class. Use `class-map match-all classname` to define a map where a packet must match all of the rules to be considered a member of the class. There are several different match rule types. The following list describes the most common types. For more discussion and examples of IPv6 QoS, consult [9]. For full details, consult the IOS QoS reference documentation [52].

- **match access-group name** *acl-name*
  This rule accepts that name of an IPv4 or IPv6 access list. To match, a packet must be permitted by the access list.

- **match packet length** [**min** *packetlen*] [**max** *packetlen*]
  This rule accepts a minimum and/or maximum packet size. To match, a packet's size must lie within the specified range (specified in bytes).

- **match protocol** *protocol-name* [*addl-parameters*]
  This rule matches a particular protocol; for some protocols, additional parameters may be supplied.

A policy map consists of a name and traffic policy definitions for one or more classes. Each class must have been defined with a class map, except for the special default-class. The structure is shown below.

```
policy-map policyname
    class classname-1
        policy-statements...
    class classname-2
        policy-statements...
        .
        .
    class class-default
    policy-statements...
```

IOS supports a large number of QoS policy statements. A few common ones are listed below. For details on all QoS features consult [52]. Each of these statements applies to a class within a policy map.

- **bandwidth** [*bw-Kbps* | **percent** *bw-percentage*]
  Reserves a portion of the interface bandwidth for traffic in the class, in kilobits per second, or as a percentage of raw interface bandwidth. This is usable only for output policy.

- **police** *bps* [*normal-burst-bps*] [*excess-burst-bps*]
     conform-action *action*
     exceed-action *action*
  This statement imposes traffic policing (similar to committed access rate). The traffic rates are in bits-per-second. Available actions include **transmit**, **drop**, and a variety of specialized keywords.

- **drop**
  This statement says to simply drop packets in the class.

Rate-Limiting Example

To illustrate the commands used for rate-limiting, the rest of this sub-section will present an extended example for the router North.

Step 1: Design the Policy Goals

This policy will have two basic goals: regulating certain application traffic, and limiting ICMPv6 traffic. Specifically, our policy will contain the following main goals.

- Reserve 15% of the output bandwidth for VoIP and related traffic. (UDP packets less than 300 bytes in length – this would need more detailed qualification in practice, but it will do for this example.)

- Limit inbound web traffic from remote servers to a maximum sustained rate of 2.5 Mbps, with bursts to 5 Mbps. (TCP source ports 80 and 443)

- Limit inbound and outbound ICMPv6 traffic to at most 200 Kbps, with bursts to 300 Kbps.

It is important to note that rate-limiting is applied per interface, therefore traffic of all protocols gets limited together. This is quite sensible, because they share the same limited bandwidth through the interface. To show how to apply rate-limiting to both IPv4 and IPv6, the rest of this example will apply the web traffic limits to IPv4 and IPv6 together.

Step 2: Define Classes

First, we need to define a traffic class for each of the kinds of traffic listed in our policy. We'll call the classes "voip-class", "web-class", and "icmp6-class". Setting up the VoIP class is shown below.

```
North# config t
Enter configuration commands, one per line. End with CNTL/Z
North(config)# ipv6 access-list voip-class-acl
North(config-ipv6-acl) permit udp any any
North(config-ipv6-acl) exit
North(config)# class-map match-all voip-class
North(config-cmap)# match access-group name voip-class-acl
North(config-cmap)# match packet length max 300
North(config-cmap)# exit
```

Setting up the web class is shown next.

```
North(config)# ipv6 access-list web-class-acl6
North(config-ipv6-acl)# permit tcp any eq www any
North(config-ipv6-acl)# permit tcp any eq 443 any
North(config-ipv6-acl)# exit
North(config)# ip access-list extended web-class-acl4
North(config-ext-nacl)# permit tcp any eq www any
North(config-ext-nacl)# permit tcp any eq 443 any
North(config-ext-nacl)# exit
North(config)# class-map match-any web-class
North(config-cmap)# match access-group name web-class-acl6
North(config-cmap)# match access-group name web-class-acl4
North(config-cmap)# exit
```

Setting up the ICMPv6 class is shown next.

```
North(config)# ipv6 access-list icmp6-class-acl
North(config-ipv6-acl)# permit icmp any any
North(config-ipv6-acl)# exit
North(config)# class-map match-all icmp6-class
North(config-cmap)# match access-group name icmp6-class-acl
North(config-cmap)# exit
North(config)#
```

Step 3: Define Policies

Having set up the various classes needed to satisfy our policy goals, we must set up policy maps for each interface and each direction of traffic. For this example, we will need two policy maps: one for outbound traffic on North's eth0 interface, and one for inbound traffic on eth0.

The transcript below shows how to set up the policy definitions for the example policy from Step 1.

```
North(config)# policy-map inet-policy-in-example
North(config-pmap)# description Inbound Internet QoS policy
North(config-pmap)# class icmp6-class
North(config-pmap-c)# police 200000 300000
North(config-pmap-c-police)# conform-action transmit
North(config-pmap-c-police)# exceed-action drop
North(config-pmap-c-police)# exit
North(config-pmap-c)# exit
North(config-pmap)# class web-class
North(config-pmap-c)# police 2500000 5000000
North(config-pmap-c-police)# conform-action transmit
North(config-pmap-c-police)# exceed-action drop
North(config-pmap-c-police)# exit
North(config-pmap-c)# exit
North(config-pmap)# exit
North(config)#
North(config)# policy-map inet-policy-out-example
North(config-pmap)# description Outbound Internet QoS policy
North(config-pmap)# class voip-class
North(config-pmap-c)# bandwidth percent 15
North(config-pmap-c)# exit
North(config-pmap)# class icmp6-class
North(config-pmap-c)# police 200000 300000
North(config-pmap-c-police)# conform-action transmit
North(config-pmap-c-police)# exceed-action drop
North(config-pmap-c-police)# exit
North(config-pmap-c)# exit
North(config-pmap)# exit
North(config)#
```

Step 4: Apply Policies

To impose the defined rate-limiting policy to traffic on an interface, use the
service-policy command as shown below.

```
North(config)# interface eth0
North(config-if)# service-policy input inet-policy-in-example
North(config-if)# service-policy output inet-policy-out-example
North(config-if)# end
North#
```

Verifying Rate-Limiting Configuration

To verify the rate-limiting policy on an interface, use the **show policy** command,
and supply the interface name as shown below.

```
North# show policy-map interface eth0
 Ethernet0
   Service-policy input: inet-policy-in-example
    Class-map: icmp6-class (match-all)
         .
       .

   Service-policy output: inet-policy-out-example
       .

North#
```

Configuring Control-Plane Policing

As described in Section 2, router operations can be abstracted into three planes:
forwarding, control, and management. The forwarding plane (also called the "data"
plane) handles transit traffic crossing through the router. The management plane
consists of traffic for configuring and monitoring router operations. The control
plane consists of the routing, signaling and link management protocols. Fast and
reliable operation of the management plane and control plane is essential for
maintaining the flow of traffic through the forwarding plane.

IOS 12.3T and later support a security mechanism called Control Plane Policing
(CPP). It provides rate-limiting for the control and management planes. Using CPP,
you can protect the router's central processor from some types of flooding attacks,
reserve control plane bandwidth for critical management access, and generally
exercise control over the finite bandwidth between the router's processor and the
outside world. CPP offers effective defense for resource exhaustion attacks directed
against the router's processor.

Not all routers and IOS releases support control-plane policing. To check whether
your router supports it, try typing the configuration command **control-plane**. If
you receive an error message, then your IOS does not support CPP. The following
transcripts show the difference in behavior between two IOS releases.

CPP Not Supported	CPP Supported
| ```
East(config)# control-plane
                   ^
% Invalid input detected...
East(config)#
``` | ```
North(config)# control-plane
North(config-cp)# exit
North(config)#
``` |

Defining policy for CPP works exactly like rate-limiting, as illustrated in the previous section. You define class maps and policy maps in exactly the same way, except that CPP supports a somewhat different set of policy statements. For more information about CPP, see [53] and Section 4.3.7 of [41].

To set up CPP, follow the steps listed below.

1. Design your CPP policy goals – identify the types of control plane traffic for which you need to reserve or restrict bandwidth. Often, you'll want to consider reserving bandwidth for routing protocols and for remote management, while limiting incoming ICMP. This step is essential.

2. Define classes – for each type of traffic listed in your policy goals, create a named class map.

3. Create policies – define a policy map for incoming control plane traffic and, if required by your policy goals, outgoing traffic.

4. Apply policies – apply the policies to the control plane using the commands control-plane and service-policy.

The example below shows how to configure CPP with a very simple input policy based on source address. The policy consists of three simple classes with associated rate limits: the trusted class allows any amount of traffic, the hostile class allows no traffic, and the default class allows up to 100 packets per second of traffic.

The transcript below shows how to define the classes. The trusted class consists of our BGP peer, anything at the remote site, or anything arriving on the internal interface. The malicious class consists of all traffic from a few external address ranges. All other traffic belongs to the default class.

```
North# config t
Enter configuration commands, one per line. End with CNTL/Z
North(config)# ipv6 access-list trusted-class-acl6
North(config-ipv6-acl)# remark Allow TCP from BGP peer
North(config-ipv6-acl)# permit tcp host 2001:db8:2::1 any
North(config-ipv6-acl)# remark Allow traffic from remote site
North(config-ipv6-acl)# permit ipv6 2001:db8:20::/44 any
North(config-ipv6-acl)# exit
North(config)# ip access-list ext trusted-class-acl4
North(config-ext-nacl)# remark Allow TCP from BGP peer
North(config-ext-nacl)# permit ip host 14.6.19.2 any
North(config-ext-nacl)# exit
```

```
North(config)# class-map match-any cpp-trusted-class
North(config-cmap)# match access-group name trusted-class-acl6
North(config-cmap)# match access-group name trusted-class-acl4
North(config-cmap)# match input-interface FastEthernet1
North(config-cmap)# exit
North(config)# ipv6 access-list hostile-class-acl6
North(config-ipv6-acl)# remark list hostile networks here
North(config-ipv6-acl)# permit 2001:db8:7c1::/48 any
North(config-ipv6-acl)# exit
North(config)# class-map match-any cpp-hostile-class
North(config-cmap)# match access-group name hostile-class-acl6
North(config-cmap)# exit
North(config)#
```

The transcript below shows how to set up the policy map.

```
North(config)# policy-map cpp-policy-example
North(config-pmap)# class cpp-hostile-class
North(config-pmap-c)# drop
North(config-pmap-c)# exit
North(config-pmap)# class cpp-trusted-class
North(config-pmap-c)# exit
North(config-pmap)# class class-default
North(config-pmap-c)# police rate 100 pps
North(config-pmap-c-police)# conform-action transmit
North(config-pmap-c-police)# exceed-action drop
North(config-pmap-c-police)# exit
North(config-pmap-c)# exit
North(config-pmap)# exit
North(config)#
```

Finally, we can apply the policy to the control plane.

```
North(config)# control-plane
North(config-cp)# service-policy input cpp-policy-example
North(config-cp)# exit
North(config)# exit
North#
```

To verify the CPP settings, use the command show policy-map control-plane.
It lists the applied policy, along with packet counts and statistics.

```
North# show policy-map control-plane
Control Plane
  Service-policy input: cpp-policy-example
    Class-map: cpp-hostile-class (match-any)
       .
        .
    Class-map: cpp-trusted-class (match-any)
      3 packets, 545 bytes
      5 minute offered rate 0 bps
      Match: access-group name cpp-trusted-acl6
        0 packets, 0 bytes
        5 minute rate 0 bps
```

```
          Match: access-group name cpp-trusted-acl4
             0 packets, 0 bytes
             5 minute rate 0 bps
          Match: input-interface FastEthernet1
             3 packets, 545 bytes
             5 minute rate 0 bps
        Class-map: class-default (match-any)
          .
            .
              .
      North#
```

3.5. Inspecting IPv6 Status and Operating Statistics

IOS offers a great many commands for examining the static IPv6 configuration and IPv6 dynamic state. Most of them begin with the keywords `show ipv6`.

Knowing the normal operating state of your network is essential to being able to troubleshoot router problems and recognize incipient attacks. The commands described below will help you extract operational IPv6 information from your routers.

<u>View Interface Configurations</u>

To view the IPv6 interface configuration, use the command `show ipv6 interface`. Add the interface name to get details about that interface only, or add the keyword `brief` to get a summary listing.

```
Central# show ipv6 interface brief
FastEthernet0/0                 [up/up]
    2001:db8:60:0:0:0:f14b:65a1
FastEthernet0/1                 [up/up]
    2001:db8:62:0:0:0:f14b:65a1
  .
    .
Central# show ipv6 interface fast0/0
FastEthernet0/0 is up, line protocol is up
  IPv6 is enabled, link-local address FE80::20C:85FF:FE5A:AD91
  Global unicast address(es):
    2001:db8:60::f14b:65a1, subnet is 2001:db8:60:/64
  Joined group address(es):
    FF02::1
    FF02::2
    FF02::1:FF5A:AD91
  MTU is 1500 bytes
  ICMP error messages limited to one every 500 milliseconds
  ICMP redirects are disabled
  .
    .
Central#
```

View Traffic Statistics

To view IPv6 traffic statistics for the whole router, use the **show ipv6 traffic** command.

```
Central# show ipv6 traffic
IPv6 statistics:
  Rcvd:  158 total, 131 local destination
         .
         .

         4 unicast RPF drop, 0 suppressed RPF drop
  Sent:  269 generated, 1 forwarded
         0 fragmented into 0 fragments, 0 failed
         0 encapsulation failed, 0 no route, 0 too big
  Mcast: 8 received, 104 sent
ICMP statistics:
  Rcvd: 349 input, 0 checksum errors, 0 too short
         .
         .

  Sent: 728 output, 0 rate-limited
         .
         .

UDP statistics:
  Rcvd: 0 input, 0 checksum errors, 0 length errors
         0 no port, 0 dropped
  Sent: 0 output
TCP statistics:
  Rcvd: 15391 input, 0 checksum errors
  Sent: 14422 output, 0 retransmitted
Central#
```

Interface accounting gives you a summary of the protocol traffic on an interface.

```
Central# show interface Fast1 accounting
FastEthernet1
        Protocol    Pkts In    Chars In    Pkts Out    Chars Out
           Other          0           0         724        43440
              IP        188       16920         191        17139
             ARP        114        6840         121         7260
            IPv6        314       91148         376        98092
Central#
```

View Routes

To examine current routes, use the **show ipv6 route** command. The summary table will show each individual route, and how it came to be in the routing table.

```
Central# show ipv6 route
IPv6 Routing Table - 18 entries
Codes: C - Connected, L - Local, S - Static, R - RIP, B - BGP
       U - Per-user Static route
       I1 - ISIS L1, I2 - ISIS L2, IA - ISIS interarea ...
       O - OSPF intra, OI - OSPF inter, OE1 - OSPF ext 1 ...
       ON1 - OSPF NSSA ext 1, ON2 - OSPF NSSA ext 2
S    ::/0 [250/0]
```

```
          via 2001:db8:60::e135:6ba4
R    2001:db8:63::/64 [120/2]
          via FE80::205:32FF:FE46:5A11, FastEthernet0/1
R    2001:db8:64::/64 [120/2]
          via FE80::205:32FF:FE46:5A11, FastEthernet0/1
I1   2001:db8:61::/64 [90/30]
          via FE80::212:1EFF:FE2E:F800, FastEthernet0/0
C    2001:db8:60::/64 [0/0]
          via ::, FastEthernet0/0
L    2001:db8:60:f14b:65a1/128 [0/0]
          via ::, FastEthernet0/0
C    2001:db8:62::/64 [0/0]
          via ::, FastEthernet0/1
L    2001:db8:62::f14b:65a1/128 [0/0]
          via ::, FastEthernet0/1
R    2001:db8:6d::43a9:3ffc/128 [120/2]
          via FE80::205:32FF:FE46:5A11, FastEthernet0/1
I1   2001:db8:6d::a32d:761f/128 [90/20]
          via FE80::212:1EFF:FE2E:F800, FastEthernet0/0

          .
LC   2001:db8:6d::ee15:f00d/128 [0/0]
          via ::, Loopback0
L    FE80::/10 [0/0]
          via ::, Null0
L    FF00::/8 [0/0]
          via ::, Null0
Central#
```

You should always be aware of the routing protocols expected in your network, and the networks they serve. If you see an unexpected routing protocol in your table, or a long list of highly specific static routes when you don't use static routes, then you know the router has been compromised.

Viewing the routing table is an important diagnostic tool, but only one of the tools you'll need to troubleshoot routing problems. Remember the following points when configuring or troubleshooting IPv6 routing.

- The router will always pick the most specific IPv6 route for forwarding packets. If you have a route to 2001:db8::/32 and a different route to 2001:db8:20::/48, the latter will always be used for packets to any host on the 2001:db8:20::/64 network.

- If a route doesn't appear in the table, then it will not be used for forwarding traffic.

- Access lists do not affect routing; if there are two paths to another network, but one of them blocks certain traffic, that will not prevent the router from attempting to send that traffic via that path. (To a limited extent, it is possible to route different kinds of traffic differently using policy-based routing, but that is beyond the scope of this document.)

- Each routing protocol maintains its own internal routing information base, but only the route with the lowest administrative distance for a particular destination gets into the main routing table. There are commands for each routing protocol that can show you those databases. The commands are:

Protocol	Command
RIPng	`show ipv6 rip database`
OSPFv3	`show ipv6 ospf`
IS-IS	`show isis ipv6 rib`
EIGRP	`show ipv6 eigrp topology`
BGP	`show bgp ipv6 unicast neighbor` *neighbor-address* **routes**

View Access Lists and Access List Counts

To examine your IPv6 access lists and their match counts, use the `show ipv6 access-list` command. You can view only a specific ACL by appending its name to the command.

```
Central# show ipv6 access-list
IPv6 access list ex2-outbound-20051122-01
    deny ipv6 FEC0::/10 any log-input sequence 10
    deny ipv6 any FEC0::/10 log-input sequence 20
    deny ipv6 any any undetermined-transport sequence 30
    permit ipv6 any FF02::/16 sequence 40
    deny ipv6 any FF00::/8 log-input sequence 50
    deny ipv6 any any log-input routing sequence 60
    permit tcp any any eq www (65084 matches) sequence 70
    permit tcp any any eq 22 (3841 matches) sequence 75
    permit tcp any any eq 443 sequence 80
    permit tcp any any eq domain sequence 90
    permit udp any any eq domain sequence 100
    permit tcp host 2001:DB8:60::45 any eq smtp sequence 110
    deny icmp any any echo-reply log-input sequence 120
    permit icmp any any sequence 130
IPv6 access list voip-class-acl
    permit udp any any sequence 10
    .       .

Central#
```

View the Neighbor Cache

The neighbor cache is a table of mappings from IPv6 addresses to link-layer (MAC) addresses. It is roughly equivalent to the ARP table for IPv4. Examining the neighbor cache can be useful for troubleshooting connectivity issues.

```
Central# show ipv6 neighbor
IPv6 Address                    Age Link-layer Addr State Interface
```

```
2001:db8:60::4                    1 0012.1e2e.f800   REACH Fa0/0
2001:db8:60:20B:DBFF:FE87:8E56    8 000b.db87.8e56   STALE Fa0/0
2001:db8:62::1F:D1B5              0 0205.3246.5a10   REACH Fa0/1
FE80::20B:DBFF:FE87:8E56          2 000b.db87.8e56   REACH Fa0/0
       .
          .
Central#
```

Each interface maintains its own neighbor cache; you can view the contents of a single cache by supplying the interface name at the end of the command.

3.6. Configuring Tunnels

In some cases, an enterprise or site network using IPv6 may not have direct connectivity to the IPv6 Internet (or other wide-area IPv6 network). Encapsulation is a transition mechanism designed to support IPv6 operations over other networks, particularly IPv4 networks.

This section covers two kinds of tunnels, manually configured tunnels, and automatic "6to4" tunnels. Cisco IOS also supports several other tunnel types; for details see [2], [9], and [42]. For an introduction to IPv6 tunnels in general, consult [1]-[5]; for an overview of IOS tunnel features, see [54]. Note that inclusion of two particular tunnel types in this document is not a recommendation to consider or use only those standards; your organization must select the right IPv6 migration mechanisms for your needs and network architecture.

There are several key security principles to remember for tunnels.

- Tunnels use encapsulation, which means that they can bypass traffic filters on physical interfaces. Always apply appropriate traffic filtering to the tunnel interface.

- Once you've configured a tunnel, it behaves like any other interface. In particular, it may be used as a route and advertised over routing protocols. Only advertise routes via tunnels that you intend to offer as a service.

- By default, tunnels do not provide integrity or confidentiality assurance. When creating a tunnel between two trusted networks over an untrusted network, such as the Internet, always use IPSec to protect the tunnel and prevent traffic injection. (IPSec is covered in Section 4.2.)

3.6.1. Creating Configured Tunnels

An IPv6 over IPv4 configured tunnel consists of two endpoints, each explicitly configured with the IPv4 address of the other. IPv6 packets from one network are encapsulated as IPv4 packet payloads. Figure 19, below, shows how a packet travels from network A to network B over a configured tunnel.

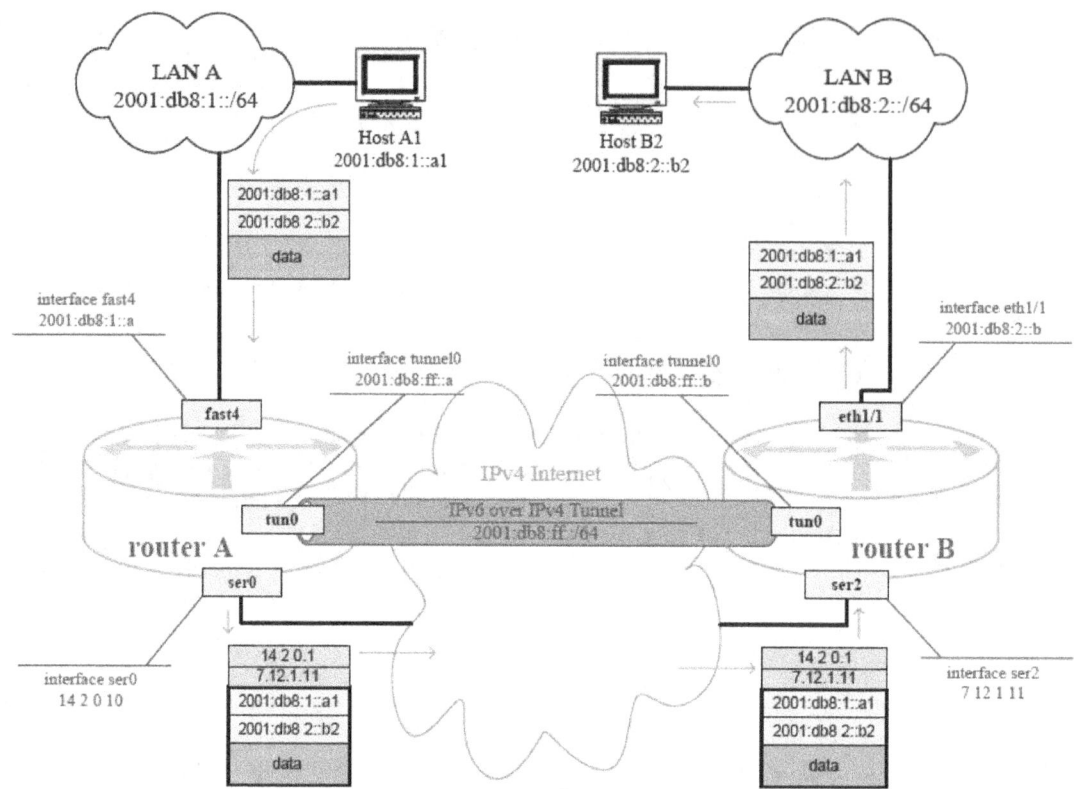

Figure 19: Operation of a Configured Tunnel

Setting up a configured tunnel simply requires two steps: creating the access lists to filter the tunnel traffic, then configuring the tunnel interface. These steps must be performed individually on each tunnel endpoint router. In general you should create access lists for your tunnel interfaces that restrict the traffic to exactly those networks which should be using the tunnel. (IPv6 Access lists are covered in Section 3.3, see page 37.)

Before configuring the tunnel on either router, you must select a network prefix for the tunnel link. In Figure 19, the prefix is 2001:db8:ff::/64. Each tunnel endpoint must have an IPv6 address with the selected prefix.

The command sequence to set up a configured tunnel is shown below.

1. Enter interface configuration mode for the tunnel interface.
    Syntax: `interface tunnel`*NN*

2. Set the tunnel mode to "ipv6ip" for raw IPv6-in-IPv4 encapsulation, or "gre ip" for Generic Routing Encapsulation (GRE).
    Syntax: `tunnel mode` *mode*

3. Set the tunnel's IPv6 address.
    Syntax: `ipv6 address` *tunnel-addr*

4. Apply the access lists, inbound and outbound.
    Syntax: `ipv6 traffic-filter` *acl-name* [`in` | `out`]

5. Set the tunnel's source interface (an IPv4 interface).
    Syntax: `tunnel source` *interface-name*

6. Set the tunnel peer endpoint address (an IPv4 address).
    Syntax: `tunnel destination` *ip-address*

7. Exit interface configuration mode.

8. Once you have set up the tunnel, it may be necessary to create static routes to the remote network that use the tunnel interface.

Tunnel Configuration Example

The example below shows how to configure the tunnel shown in Figure 19, on routerA and routerB.

Step 1: Create Access Lists for the Tunnel

On routerA, we'll create access lists that permit traffic to and from network B only, including the tunnel address of router B. These access lists are only examples, in practice you might restrict the traffic more narrowly.

```
routerA(config)# ipv6 access-list from-B-only
routerA(config-ipv6-acl)# permit ipv6 2001:db8:2::/64
                                     2001:db8:1::/64
routerA(config-ipv6-acl)# permit ipv6 host 2001:db8:ff::b
                                     host 2001:db8:ff::a
routerA(config-ipv6-acl)# exit
routerA(config)# ipv6 access-list to-B-only
routerA(config-ipv6-acl)# permit ipv6 2001:db8:1::/64
                                     2001:db8:2::/64
routerA(config-ipv6-acl)# permit ipv6 host 2001:db8:ff::a
                                     host 2001:db8:ff::b
routerA(config-ipv6-acl)# exit
```

On routerB, we create similar access lists for this example. They do not need to match, if the operations between the two networks is restricted to certain traffic in particular directions.

```
routerB(config)# ipv6 access-list from-A-only
routerB(config-ipv6-acl)# permit ipv6 2001:db8:1::/64
                                     2001:db8:2::/64
routerB(config-ipv6-acl)# permit ipv6 host 2001:db8:ff::a
                                     host 2001:db8:ff::b
routerB(config-ipv6-acl)# exit
routerB(config)# ipv6 access-list to-A-only
routerB(config-ipv6-acl)# permit ipv6 2001:db8:2::/64
                                     2001:db8:1::/64
routerB(config-ipv6-acl)# permit ipv6 host 2001:db8:ff::b
                                     host 2001:db8:ff::a
routerB(config-ipv6-acl)# exit
```

Steps 2-7: Setting Up the Tunnel

Next, we will set up identical tunnel interfaces on each router. First, routerA with the destination set to routerB's IPv4 address.

```
routerA(config)# interface tunnel0
routerA(config-if)# tunnel mode ipv6ip
routerA(config-if)# ipv6 address 2001:db8:ff::a/64
routerA(config-if)# ipv6 traffic-filter from-B-only in
routerA(config-if)# ipv6 traffic-filter to-B-only out
routerA(config-if)# tunnel source serial0
routerA(config-if)# tunnel destination 7.12.1.11
routerA(config-if)# exit
routerA(config)#
```

Next, routerB with destination set to routerA's IPv4 address.

```
routerB(config)# interface tunnel0
routerB(config-if)# tunnel mode ipv6ip
routerB(config-if)# ipv6 address 2001:db8:ff::b/64
routerB(config-if)# ipv6 traffic-filter from-A-only in
routerB(config-if)# ipv6 traffic-filter to-A-only out
routerB(config-if)# tunnel source serial2
routerB(config-if)# tunnel destination 14.1.0.10
routerB(config-if)# exit
routerB(config)#
```

At this point, the tunnel is active. Test it using the ping command.

```
routerA(config)# do ping 2001:db8:ff::b
Type escape sequence to abort.
Sending 5, 100-byte ICMP Echos to 2001:DB8:FF::b, ...
!!!!!
Success rate is 100 percent (5/5), round-trip ...
routerA(config)#
```

The ping command shows that the tunnel is up, but hosts on network A will not be able to reach network B yet.

Step 8: Add Static Routes

To allow hosts on network A to use the tunnel for communication with network B, and vice versa, we need to add a static route to the peer network on each router.

```
routerA(config)# ipv6 route 2001:db8:2::/64 2001:db8:ff::b
routerA(config)# exit
```

And on routerB:

```
routerB(config)# ipv6 route 2001:db8:1::/64 2001:db8:ff::a
routerB(config)# exit
```

Tunnel Encapsulation Modes

IOS supports many different encapsulation modes for tunnels. The two most appropriate modes for linking IPv6 enclaves over an IPv4 network are IPv6-in-IP (ipv6ip) and GRE. The picture at right shows how the encapsulations compare.

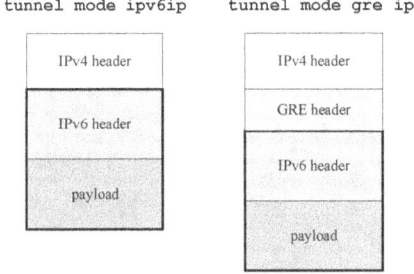

GRE encapsulation offers some additional flexibilty, but imposes a little more overhead. GRE can be used to encapsulate multiple network layer protocols simultaneously. IS-IS can run over a GRE tunnel.

The example above shows IPv6-in-IP encapsulation, but to turn it into a GRE example, simply change the tunnel modes on each router to `tunnel mode gre ip`.

Verifying Tunnel Configuration

To view the tunnel configuration and traffic statistics, use the `show interface` command as illustrated below.

```
routerA# show interface tunnel0
Tunnel0 is up, line protocol is up
  Hardware is Tunnel
  MTU 1514 bytes, BW 9 Kbit, DLY 500000 usec,
      reliability 255/255, txload 1/255, rxload 1/255
  Encapsulation TUNNEL, loopback not set
  Keepalive not set
  Tunnel source 14.2.0.10 (Serial0), destination 7.12.1.11
  Tunnel protocol/transport IPv6/IP
      .
      .
routerA#
```

3.6.2. Configuring 6to4 Tunnels

6to4 is a form of automated tunneling designed for connecting "IPv6 domains over IPv4 clouds." It uses the IPv4 address of a router as a designator for the entire IPv6 network that the router serves. The IPv6 address is specifically structured to include the IPv4 address of the tunnel endpoint. Figure 20 shows the structure of a 6to4 address. The address prefix 2002::/16 is reserved for 6to4 tunnel endpoints.

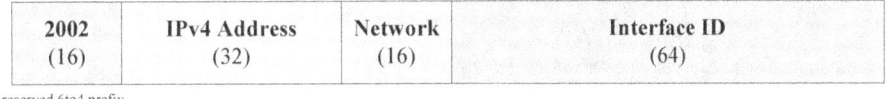

reserved 6to4 prefix

Figure 20: 6to4 Automatic Tunneling IPv6 Address

6to4 is automatic because the administrators of each router do not need to configure individual tunnels to each endpoint peer – once a router is configured with a 6to4 tunnel interface, it can (in theory) exchange encapsulated IPv6 traffic with any other 6to4 router. For more information, consult RFC 3056 [32], or the tunneling chapters of [2], [5], or [7].

How Does 6to4 Work?

6to4 is often used to connect an IPv6 or dual-stack network with IPv4 connectivity to the IPv6 Internet. Figure 21 shows an example of router Remote connecting to the IPv6 Internet through a public 6to4 gateway. Router Remote has the global IPv4 address 7.12.1.20, so its 6to4 prefix is 2002:070c:0114::/48.

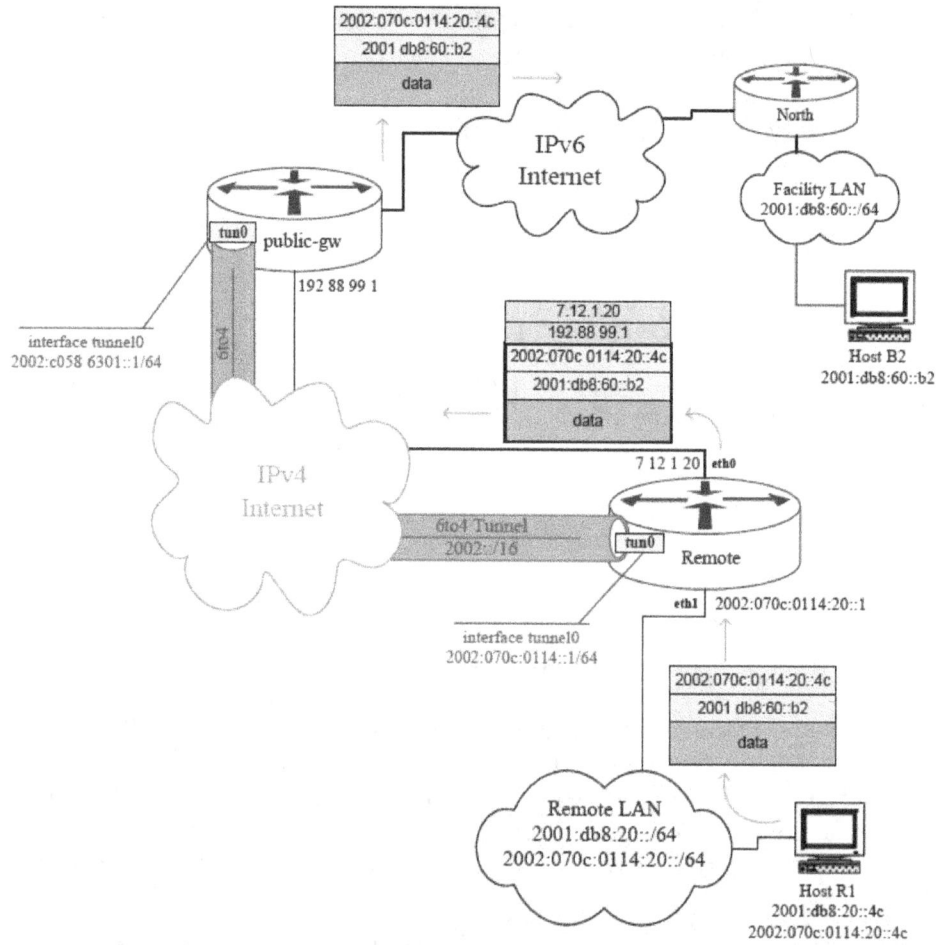

Figure 21: Operation of 6to4 Automatic Tunnels

Figure 21 shows a packet sent by host R1 being encapsulated and then routed onto the IPv6 Internet. For traffic coming back to host R1, the host must be addressable using a 6to4 address. The figure shows the Remote LAN supporting a 6to4 network address; this is usually necessary for 6to4 to work properly.

Public 6to4 relay routers exist to route packets between 6to4 networks and the IPv6 Internet. Large enterprises will probably wish to run their own 6to4 relays to exercise greater control over their traffic processing and bandwidth usage. Configuring and operating a 6to4 relay router is outside the scope of this document.

6to4 Configuration Example

The following example shows how to configure the router Remote to use a 6to4 tunnel.

Because the 6to4 tunnel will be the Remote LAN's primary link to the IPv6 Internet, it should have full IPv6 Internet traffic filtering, as recommended in Section 3.3.

```
Remote# config t
Enter configuration commands, one per line. End with CNTL/Z
Remote(config)# ipv6 access-list border6to4-inbound-ex
Remote(config-ipv6-acl)# deny ipv6  ff00::/16  any  log
  .
  .
Remote(config-ipv6-acl)# exit
Remote(config)# ipv6 access-list border6to4-outbound-ex
Remote(config-ipv6-acl)# deny ipv6  ff00::/16  any  log
  .
  .
Remote(config-ipv6-acl)# exit
Remote(config)#
```

The transcript below shows how set up the 6to4 prefix and router advertisements on the inside LAN interface of Remote.

```
Remote(config)# interface eth1
Remote(config-if)# ipv6 address 2002:070c:0114:20::1/64
Remote(config-if)# ipv6 nd prefix 2002:070c:0114:20::/64
Remote(config-if)# exit
Remote(config)#
```

Finally, set up the tunnel interface itself. The mode for a 6to4 tunnel is "ipv6ip 6to4". Note that the configuration includes a tunnel source address, but no destination address. No destination address is needed because the 6to4 IPv6 address incorporates the IPv4 destination, as shown in Figure 20.

```
Remote(config)# interface tunnel0
Remote(config-if)# no ip redirects
Remote(config-if)# tunnel mode ipv6ip 6to4
Remote(config-if)# ipv6 address 2002:070c:0114::1/64
Remote(config-if)# ipv6 traffic-filt border6to4-inbound-ex in
Remote(config-if)# ipv6 traffic-filt border6to4-outbound-ex out
Remote(config-if)# tunnel source 7.12.1.20
Remote(config-if)# keepalive 30
Remote(config-if)# exit
Remote(config)#
```

For the Remote LAN to use the 6to4 tunnel for traffic, we must also add a static route giving the IPv6 address of the remote 6to4 peer as the IPv6 default gateway.

```
Remote(config)# ipv6 route ::/0 tun0 2002:c058:6301::1
Remote(config)# exit
```

Verifying Tunnel Configuration

Use the `show interface` command to view tunnel configuration and traffic statistics.

```
Remote# show interface tunnel0
Tunnel0 is up, line protocol is up
  Hardware is Tunnel
  MTU 1514 bytes, BW 9 Kbit, DLY 500000 usec,
     reliability 255/255, txload 1/255, rxload 1/255
  Encapsulation TUNNEL, loopback not set
  Keepalive set (30 sec), retries 3
  Tunnel source 7.0.1.20, destination UNKNOWN
  Tunnel protocol/transport IPv6 6to4
    .
    .
  5 minute input rate 2000 bits/sec, 2 packets/sec
  5 minute output rate 12800 bits/sec, 11 packets/sec
     9674 packets input, 1143012 bytes, 0 no buffer
     Received 0 broadcasts, 0 runts, 0 giants, 0 throttles
     0 input errors, 0 CRC, 0 frame, 0 overrun, 0 ignored
     86182 packets output, 7679276 bytes, 0 underruns
     0 output errors, 0 collisions, 0 interface resets
     0 output buffer failures, 0 output buffers swapped out
Remote#
```

For more diagnostic commands, see Section 3.5.

4. Advanced Topics in IPv6 Security

This section covers a selection of advanced IPv6 security topics for IOS routers.

4.1. IPv6 Routing Protocol Security

IPv6 was designed as the successor to IPv4, and must be able to support very large networks and collections of networks. Routers forward packets between networks by using the contents of their internal routing table to select an output interface for each incoming packet. For a network to operate efficiently and reliably, the internal routing tables of all the routers in the network must be accurate and consistent.

In a small network, it is reasonable for administrators to explicitly configure routes to each network destination on every router. These are called static routes; the syntax for adding static routes in IOS appears in Section 3.2.5.

The static route approach has several drawbacks that make it unsuitable for modern networks.

- Lack of scalability – as the number of routers in a network grows, the number of static routes needed grows rapidly. In a network with more than 3-4 routers, the number of static routes becomes unmaintainable.

- Lack of robustness – static routes are fixed, and a router that depends on them cannot react to changes in network topology. If a particular link goes down, then all static routes dependent on that link become unusable, and traffic will be lost.

The alternative to static routes is dynamic routing, where routers exhange path and network topology information among each other using *routing protocols*. The rest of this section describes security measures for routing protocols. Use them to protect the integrity of the routing information conveyed between your routers.

Routing protocols fall into two general types: Interior Gateway Protocols (IGPs) are designed for use within an autonomous system (AS), that is, among routers that are all controlled by the same enterprise or organization. Exterior Gateway Protocols (EGPs) are designed for exchanging routes between autonomous systems, such as between network carriers or between a large enterprise and its network service providers.

For general information about IPv6 routing and routing protocols, see [2], [5], [7], [9], or [10]. For a discussion of IPv4 routing protocol security, see [6] or section 4.4 of the RSCG [41].

4.1.1. Available IPv6 Routing Protocols and Selection Issues

Several routing protocols exist for IPv6, and all IPv6-capable versions of IOS support at least some of them. The table below describes the available routing protocols.

Protocol Name	Type	Description
Routing Information Protocol (RIPng)	IGP	The IPv6 version of RIP is a simple distance vector routing protocol, standardized in RFC 2080. It is easy to configure, but offers limited flexibility and scalability. Each RIPng update contains a copy of the entire routing table. RIPng is suited for networks of modest size only.
Open Shortest Path First version 3 (OSPFv3)	IGP	OSPF version 3 is designed specifically for IPv6. It is a link-state routing protocol that offers flexibility and efficiency. Each update contains only changes to the network topology. It is suitable for IPv6 networks of any size. OSPFv3 is standardized in RFC 2740.
Intermediate-System to Intermediate System (IS-IS)	IGP	The OSI routing protocol IS-IS has been extended to support IPv4 and IPv6. The version that can support both is called "integrated IS-IS". Each IS-IS update contains only changes to the network topology. IS-IS is very flexible and efficient, and is suitable for large IPv4/v6 networks.
EIGRP for IPv6	IGP	Cisco EIGRP routing protocol was recently extended to support IPv6. It is a link-state routing protocol that offers fast convergence and efficiency. It is suitable for large IPv6 networks. EIGRP is a Cisco proprietary protocol and is only supported on Cisco IOS routers.
Border Gateway Protocol	EGP	BGP version 4 with multi-protocol extensions supports both IPv4 and IPv6. It is the routing protocol used routing between autonomous systems (AS) in the Internet. Each BGP update contains only changes to the network topology. BGP is very efficient and flexible. Multi-protocol BGP is standardized in RFC 2858.

All effective routing protocols allow your networks to adapt to changes in topology. When selecting a routing protocol for your network, you must consider several factors: availability on your routers, speed of convergence, flexibility, scalability, and security. The sub-sections below discuss each factor briefly.

Availability

Some IOS feature sets and releases support all the routing protocols listed above, but most do not.

- RIPng – all IPv6-capable IOS releases support this basic routing protocol.

- OSPFv3 – most (but not all) IPv6-capable IOS releases 12.3 and later support this highly capable routing protocol.

- IS-IS – many IPv6-capable IOS releases 12.3 and later support integrated IS-IS, but only with advanced feature sets: Advanced IP Services and Advanced Enterprise Services.

- EIGRP for IPv6 – only the very latest IOS releases, 12.4(6)T and later, support this protocol. Because EIGRP support for IPv6 is very new, it is not covered in this supplement. For information about configuring and securing EIGRP for IPv6 consult the Cisco documentation, [44] and [61].

- BGP – most IPv6-capable IOS releases 12.3 and later support BGP with multi-protocol extensions. BGP is useful only as an EGP; do not use it for general dynamic routing within an AS.

For a listing of IPv6 routing features and the releases that support them, consult [43].

Speed of Convergence

When a change occurs in your network's topology, such as a link going down or a router interface failing, there will be a delay before the routing tables on every router accurately reflect the new network state. The speed with which all the routers *converge* on the new state is an important performance criterion for routing protocols. RIPng generally has relatively slow convergence, while OSPFv3 and BGP are much faster. IS-IS offers the fastest convergence in large networks.

Flexibility and Scalability

IOS offers a wide variety of features for controlling routing and routing protocols. One important aspect of flexibility is whether the routing protocol naturally supports segmenting your network into separate parts, and managing exchange of routes among them. OSPF and IS-IS handle segmenting very well, RIPng does not.

Scalability is important for selecting a routing protocol for larger networks. RIPng has a built-in limit of 15 hops in its updates, so it cannot be used for networks where the distance between any two hosts might be more than 15. In practice, any network with more than a few dozen routers should be running OSPFv3 or IS-IS, because they offer more efficient updates and more accurate modeling of network topology.

BGP offers outstanding flexibility, but it cannot be used as an IGP. Within an AS, every iBGP router must be configured with a connection to every other BGP router ("full mesh") or specific BGP routers must be designated as route reflectors.

Security

As discussed in Section 2, the usual security threat for routing protocols is unauthorized modification. An attacker that can modify or inject routing updates can impose denial of service and possibly intercept traffic. The main security criterion for routing protocols is integrity assurance: can the routing protocol messages be protected from modification and can the protocol reject unauthorized messages?

The list below describes the security mechanisms for each protocol.

- RIPng – the IPv6 version of RIP offers no integrity assurance features. Therefore, RIPng is suitable only for small, private networks where the threat of routing attacks is negligible. (RIP for IPv4 has an MD5-based integrity mechanism, but it was removed from RIPng.)

- OSPFv3 – the IPv6 version of OSPF offers no integrity assurance features itself, but the standard recommends protecting OSPF messages with IPSec Authentication Header (AH). Many IOS releases 12.3T and later support using IPSec AH for integrity assurance of OSPFv3.

- IS-IS – this routing protocol supports a simple MD5-based integrity mechanism that uses secret keys (passwords) to validate messages. All IOS releases that support IS-IS for IPv6 also support MD5 security.

- EIGRP – Cisco's EIGRP for IPv6 supports a simple MD5-based integrity mechanism, exactly like EIGRP for IPv4.

- BGP – the use of BGP as an inter-AS routing protocol means that it is subject to serious threats. Three mechanisms exist to combat threats to BGP: an MD5-based integrity mechanism, the Generalized TTL Security Mechanism (GTSM), and IPSec.

The next section describes prefix-lists and how to create them. Subsequent sections provide recommendations and examples for securing OSPFv3, IS-IS, and BGP.

4.1.2. Prefix-Lists

All IPv6 routing protocols support mechanisms for controlling what routes are advertised, and what routes will be accepted. In most cases, you can select between two means for specifying addresses: access lists and prefix-lists. Prefix-lists are more succinct and more efficient. For more information about prefix-lists, consult [44].

An IPv6 prefix-list must be identified with a name, and consists of one or more matching rules, plus an optional description. The syntax for adding a prefix-list rule is shown below.

```
ipv6 prefix-list name [ seq seqnumber ] match-expr [ length-expr ]
```

The name can be any identifier. The sequence number must be a positive integer; rules get applied in the order of their sequence numbers. The match expression controls whether the rule permits or denies particular addresses. The syntax is:

```
{ permit | deny } ipv6-address/length
```

Finally, the optional length expression allows a rule to apply only to route prefixes whose mask length falls within a specified range. The syntax is:

```
[ ge min-length ] [ le max-length ]
```

The example rule below permits prefixes that match 2001:db8::/32, but are at least 48 bits long. The example also shows how to set a prefix-list description.

```
ipv6 prefix-list testList description A small example list
ipv6 prefix-list testList seq 10 permit 2001:db8::/32 ge 48
```

If you want to create rules that only restrict the lengths of prefixes, use the ::/0 in the match expression.

The example below shows how to create a prefix-list, and how to inspect it. Always inspect your prefix-lists for accuracy after creating them. The example list permits the routes to the portion of the sample network served by the router South, and denies all other routes.

```
        config t
      ipv6 prefix-list southern description South routes
      ipv6 prefix-list southern seq 20
             permit 2001:db8:63::/64 ge 64
      ipv6 prefix-list southern seq 30
             permit 2001:db8:64::/64 ge 64
      ipv6 prefix-list southern seq 99 deny ::/0 le 128
      exit
   show ipv6 prefix-list
```

4.1.3. Securing OSPFv3

The OSPFv3 protocol does not include any security features of its own. Instead, it depends on the IPSec Authentication Header (AH) protocol to protect its messages. IOS 12.3T and later support AH protection for OSPFv3.

OSPFv3 deployment in a network is divided into areas, and every deployment must have a backbone area, number 0. OSPFv3 IPSec integrity assurance can be configured on a per-link or per-area basis. Because illicit updates can propagate through OSPF, it is best to configure IPSec protection on a per-area basis, and use a distinct key for each area.

OSPFv3 for IPv6 and OSPFv2 for IPv4 are completely separate and independent. Protecting one of them offers no protection for the other.

Deployment of OSPF in a large network is complicated, and outside the scope of this document. Numerous books and Cisco whitepapers cover OSPF for IPv4, the strategies and principles discussed in them are generally applicable to IPv6 as well. For more information, see Sections 4.4.3 and 4.4.8 of the RSCG [41].

Configuring OSPFv3 with IPSec Authentication

To configure IPSec-authenticated OSPFv3 for a router in an area, follow the steps listed below.

1. Configure the OSPFv3 routing process.

2. Define an IPSec Security Parameter Index (SPI) and HMAC key for each OSPF area in which the router will participate.

3. Configure OSPF for IPv6 on each IPv6 interface that will exchange updates with other OSPFv3 routers. (Note: OSPFv3 runs only on IPv6.)

OSPFv3 Configuration Example

For this example, we will configure two OSPF areas in our simple network. Router Central participates in the backbone area (area 0) and in the southern area (area 1).

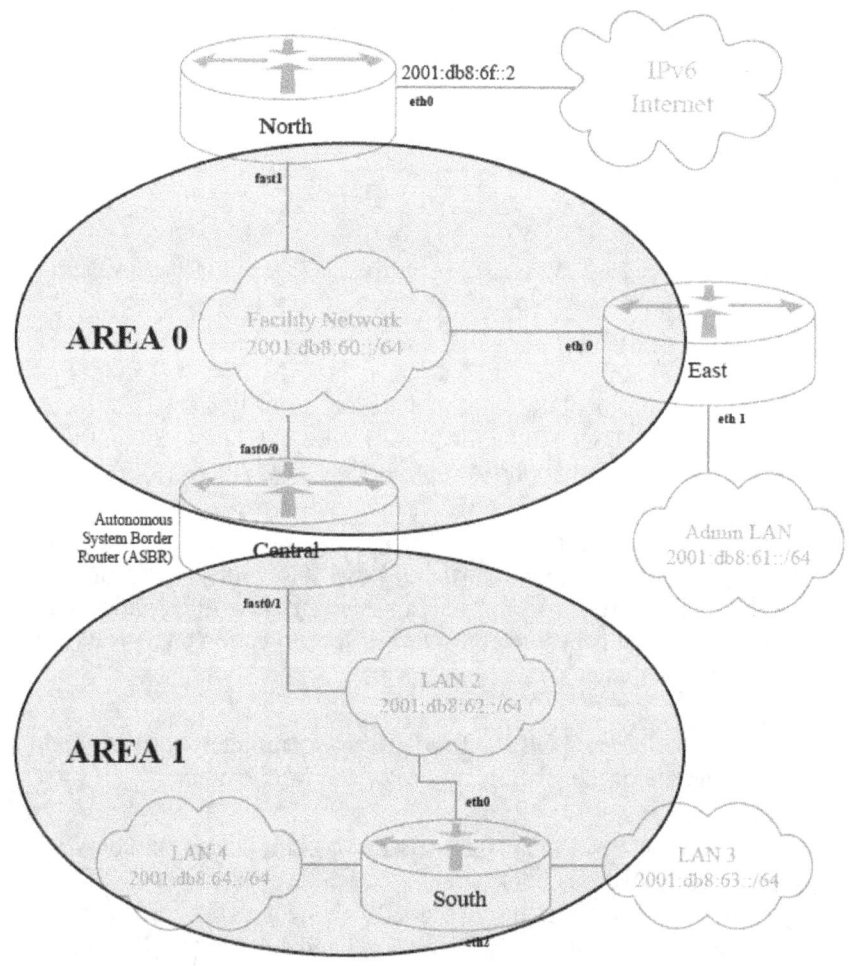

Figure 22: Example OSPFv3 Areas

(Of course, our example network is too small to need two OSPF areas, it is broken up in this way just to illustrate configuring two separate areas.)

First, we'll create the routing process for OSPFv3. The transcript below shows how to start an OSPFv3 routing process and configure it to advertise routes to connected links. (Note use of the `router-id` command to assign a unique 32-bit ID required for OSPF.)

```
           config t
      ...................... ........... .... .... ..... .... .... ..../.
                      ipv6 router ospf 1
                        redistribute connected
                         router-id 14.1.0.251
```

Next, we'll define the IPSec AH keys and SPI to use for each OSPF area. IOS 12.3T and later support IPSec AH for OSPF, but they require you to enter a raw MD5 or SHA-1 HMAC key manually. The transcript below shows how to set up IPSec for router Central's two areas.

```
                       area 0 authentication ipsec spi 520
           md5 0 b0c158012fa552f817d536a8121b388
                      area 1 authentication ipsec spi 521
           md5 0 a07bec7208c01e390f7d60c9488f2e83
                       exit
```

Finally, we enable OSPFv3 on the router's interfaces.

```
                    interface fast0/0
                      description Facility LAN, OSPF area 0
                     ipv6 ospf 1 area 0
                    exit
                   interface fast0/1
                      description LAN 2, OSPF area 1
                     ipv6 ospf 1 area 1
                    exit
                  exit
```

Of course, the routers North and East must be configured with the area 0 key, and the router South with the area 1 key, before OSPFv3 updates can be sent among them.

Generating OSPFv3 IPSec Keys

Raw keys are difficult to remember, because they must be entered as hexadecimal strings of exact length. Good passwords are easier to select, distribute to colleagues, and remember. You can use the Unix/Linux **md5sum(1)** utility to convert a good password into a hexadecimal MD5 string for OSPFv3 IPSec configuration. The command transcript below (performed on Linux) shows how to use md5sum.

```
  echo "r0utes4all++" | md5sum
```

The hexadecimal string output from md5sum may be pasted directly onto the OSPFv3 area authentication command.

4.1.4. Securing IS-IS

IS-IS is a link-state routing protocol originally standardized by the International Standards Organization (ISO) for supporting ISO networks. The IETF adapted it to IPv4 routing and, later, IPv6. IS-IS provides a two-level hierarchy for managing network routes: level 2 corresponds to the OSPF "backbone" area, and level 1 corresponds roughly to OSPF stub areas. You can run IS-IS with just level 2 for small and medium sized networks; only with a large network will you need level 1.

Because it was designed by ISO, IS-IS does not run over IP or IPv6, it runs on the ISO Connectionless Network Service (CLNS). Because IP routers do not forward CLNS packets, it is virtually impossible for an external attacker to inject IS-IS messages onto your network. To prevent local attackers from corrupting or injecting routing updates, IS-IS supports password authentication. IS-IS supports both plaintext and MD5-based password authentication. Use only the MD5-based authentication.

On IOS routers, IS-IS uses the "key chain" mechanism for managing passwords. This is a very flexible and effective facility that allows periodic rotation of passwords without disrupting service. (EIGRP for IPv6 uses the key chain mechanism for its authentication passwords, too.)

IOS routers that support IS-IS and IPv6 allow four kinds of IS-IS operation.

- IPv4 only – see Section 4.4.3 of the RSCG [41] for instructions on securing IS-IS for IPv4.

- IPv6 only – in this mode of operation, the IS-IS messages carry only IPv6 routes.

- IPv4 and IPv6 – in this mode of operation, the IS-IS messages carry IPv4 and IPv6 network updates, but the topologies of IPv4 connectivity and IPv6 connectivity must match.

- Multi-topology – in this mode of operation, IS-IS messages carry both IPv4 and IPv6 routes. The network topologies do not need to match.

It is also possible to run two separate IS-IS routing processes, and run the IPv4 and IPv6 processes separately. This may be advantageous if the IPv4 IS-IS deployment is already running and you don't want to risk disrupting it.

IS-IS is not trivial to set up, but once working it is not difficult to manage. The community consensus seems to be that IS-IS is best suited for large networks where scalability and speed of convergence are paramount concerns.

Checking for IS-IS Support

IS-IS support for IPv6 was added in IOS 12.2T, but only the more complete IOS feature packs support IS-IS. To check whether your IOS image has IS-IS, type the configuration command `router isis` as shown below. You can see whether the IS-IS support includes IPv6 by checking the `address-family` command, shown below on the right.

IS-IS Not Supported	IS-IS Supported
☐☐☐☐☐☐☐☐☐☐☐☐☐ `router isis 1` ☐☐☐☐☐☐☐☐☐ ☐☐☐ ☐☐ ☐☐☐☐ ☐☐☐☐☐ ☐☐☐☐☐☐☐☐☐☐☐☐☐☐	☐☐☐☐☐☐☐☐☐☐☐☐☐`router isis 1` ☐☐☐☐☐☐☐☐☐☐☐☐☐☐☐☐☐ `address-family ?` ☐☐☐☐ ☐☐☐☐☐☐☐ ☐☐☐☐☐☐ ☐☐☐☐☐☐☐☐☐☐☐☐☐☐☐☐☐ `address-family^C` ☐☐☐☐☐

Configuring Multi-Topology IS-IS with MD5 Authentication

To configure IS-IS with MD5 password authentication for both IPv4 and IPv6, follow the steps listed below.

1. Create a key chain for IS-IS, and populate it with one or more keys. Each key can have an associated key lifetime (see below). Keys can be any length – make them long and hard to guess.

2. Configure the IS-IS routing process. This requires several sub-steps:

   - Assign an ISO Network Entity Title (the title must have the form ☐☐☐☐☐☐☐☐$xxxx$☐$yyyy$☐$zzzz$☐☐☐ and each router must have its own title).
   - Set the IS type to level 2.
   - Set the metric style to "wide" for level 2.
   - Set the authentication mode and key chain for level 2.
   - Enable multi-topology operation for the IPv6 address family. (This is optional if your IPv4 and IPv6 networks have exactly the same connection topology. If in doubt, enable multi-topology operation.)
   - Enable redistribution of connected networks and other routing protocols into IS-IS level 2 [optional].

3. For each interface that will support IS-IS, set the authentication mode and key chain, then enable IS-IS operation.

The steps above assume that you jump right in to multi-topology IS-IS. If you want to set up IS-IS for IPv6 only, or migrate from IS-IS for IPv4 to integrated IS-IS, consult section 6.5 of [10], or the "Implementing IS-IS" section of [42]. For more information about IS-IS in general, consult [59].

IS-IS Configuration Example

For this example, we will configure multi-topology IS-IS on the facility LAN of our simple network. The router Central also performs RIPng routing with the router South, because South does not support IS-IS.

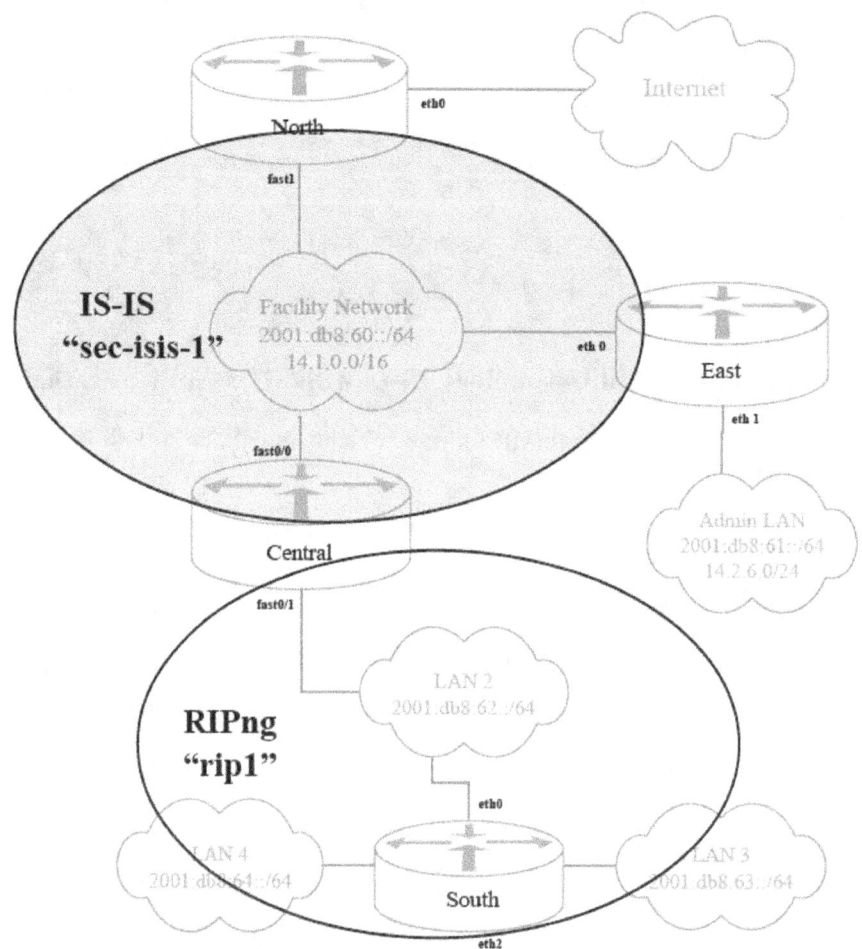

Figure 23: Example IS-IS Configuration

First, configure a key chain. In this example, we provide two keys, each good for about three months, offset by a month. The `accept-lifetime` command specifies the interval during which the key will be accepted for authentication by IS-IS peers, and the `send-lifetime` command specifies the interval during which this router may use the key for authenticating outgoing messages. Each month administrators can go through and add a new key and delete any obsolete keys.

```
Central# config t
Enter configuration commands, one per line. End with CNTL/Z
Central(config)# key chain ISIS-KC
Central(config-keychain)# key 1
```

```
                                       key-string 6tfhdnn48+23sk
                                       accept-life 0:0:0 1 Dec 2005
                                                   0:0:0 1 Mar 2006
                                       send-life   0:0:0 1 Dec 2005
                                                   0:0:0 1 Feb 2006
                                   exit
                              key 2
                                   key-string I6imfp-y2k+XYZ
                                   accept-life 0:0:0 1 Jan 2006
                                               0:0:0 1 Apr 2006
                                   send-life   0:0:0 1 Jan 2006
                                               0:0:0 1 Mar 2006
                              exit
                         exit
```

Next, configure the IS-IS routing process. IOS can support several independent IS-IS processes, each with its own name. In this example, we'll use the name "sec-isis-1".

```
              router isis sec-isis-1
               ! set network entity title
               net 49.0001.0060.ee15.f00d.00
               ! set level to 1, configure level 2
               is-type level-2-only
               authentication mode md5 level-2
               authentication key-chain ISIS-KC level-2
               metric-syle wide level-2
               redistribute connected level-2
               ! configure IPv6 support
               address-family ipv6
               ! using multi-topology is optional
                multi-topology
                redistribute rip rip-1 level-2
                       include-connected
                redistribute connected level-2
                exit-address-family
               exit
```

Finally, we can enable IS-IS on the appropriate interface(s).

```
              interface fast0/0
               isis authentication mode md5 level-2
               isis authentication key-chain ISIS-KC
                                    level-2
               isis ipv6 metric 20
               ip router isis sec-isis-1
               ipv6 router isis sec-isis-1
               exit
             exit
```

Of course, routers North and East would have to be configured in a very similar fashion, although without the line for redistributing RIPng routes.

For more examples of configuring IS-IS for IPv6, consult [5] and [42].

Verifying IS-IS Operation

To check that IS-IS is operating, use the `show isis` command as illustrated below. Each nearby IS-IS router should appear on the neighbors listing. Routes obtained via IS-IS will appear on the RIB listing.

```
□□□□□□□□ show isis neighbors

□□□□□□□ □□   □□□□ □□□□□□□□□  □□ □□□□□□□   □□□□□ □□□□□□□□□ □□□□□□□ □□
□□□□          □□  □□□/□      □□□□□□□□□□□  □□   □          □□□□□□□□
□□□□□□        □□  □□□/□      □□□□□□□□□□□□ □□   □□          □□□□□□□□
□□□□□□□□□□
□□□□□□□□ show isis ipv6 rib
□ □□□□□□□□□□□□□□□/□□
    □□□ □□□□□□□□□□□□□□□□□□□□□□□/□□□□□□□□□□□□□/□□ □□□□ □□ □□□□□□ □□
□ □□□□□□□□□□□□□□□/□□
    □□□ □□□□□□□□□□□□□□□□□□□□□□□/□□□□□□□□□□□□□/□□ □□□□ □□ □□□□□□ □□
      □
        □
□□□□□□□□□
```

For details of commands for inspecting IS-IS operation and routes for IPv6, consult the IOS *IPv6 Command Reference* [44].

4.1.5. Securing BGP for IPv6

Multi-protocol BGP is the exterior gateway protocol for the Internet. It is capable of carrying both IPv4 and IPv6 routes between routers, efficiently and reliably. In this section, all uses of the acronym "BGP" refer to multi-protocol BGP, as defined in RFC 2858 [21].

BGP sessions are TCP connections, BGP can run over IPv4 or IPv6. This section will show examples of configuring BGP neighbors using both IPv4 and IPv6.

Typically, network service providers use BGP to exchange routes between their autonomous systems. BGP can also be used within an AS for carrying exterior (Internet) routes among BGP routers at the edges of the AS network; when used in this fashion, it is called iBGP. Deployment and operation of BGP in an Internet context is very complex, and far beyond the scope of this supplement. For more information about BGP operations, consult [8] and [10].

The main security objectives for BGP are integrity for the routing updates, and availability of the BGP service. An extensive and detailed analysis of BGP threats and vulnerabilities appears in RFC 4272 [33]. For this section, we will worry about two main threats and countermeasures against them: (1) unauthorized routing table modifications, and (2) denial of service, meaning disruption or prevention of BGP peering sessions.

The interior gateway protocols described earlier in this section are used only for distributing routes within your network; BGP is used to exchange routes with the rest of the world's networks. Operationally, it can be very important to control what routes you advertise via BGP, and which routes you accept from BGP peers. You can use a prefix-list to control what routes you advertise, and another to control what routes you accept.

BGP Integrity and Availability Assurance Mechanisms

There are several standard security mechanisms available for BGP. All of them work for both IPv4 and IPv6.

Mechanism	Description	Effective for	
		(1)	(2)
TCP MD5 Signature	Uses a static secret password to authenticate BGP peers and validate BGP messages. Described in RFC 2385.	yes	partial
GTSM	The Generalized TTL Security Mechanism discourages remote attacks by enforcing a TTL lower bound on incoming BGP TCP packets. Described in RFC 3682.	partial	partial
IPSec	Protect BGP traffic using a router-to-router IPSec connection, based on AH or ESP.	yes	yes

The MD5 Signature mechanism requires administrators to configure each peer router with a static shared secret or password. That secret is combined with the MD5 hash of each BGP TCP packet, and sent as a TCP option. The receiving router must recompute the hash and drop any packets for which the check fails. This mechanism is effective at rejecting malicious injection and modification of BGP messages, but requires manual provisioning of secrets on each peer router. Effective security using a fixed secret value of this kind requires updating the secret regularly.

In typical applications, external BGP peer routers are directly connected, or the number of layer 3 hops between them is fixed, well-known, and small. For example, BGP peer routers at two ISPs might be connected directly by an ATM link. GTSM is a very simple security mechanism for rejecting spoofed BGP messages based on their IP TTL or Hop Limit. The sending BGP router always uses a TTL=255, and the receiving BGP router checks that the TTL has the expected value of 255 or 255-*hops*. Any packets from a remote attacker would have to travel over through more intervening routers, and would therefore have a lower-than-required TTL, and would be dropped on receipt. If an attacker can co-opt a node on the path between the routers, GTSM is ineffective.

IPSec is the standard mechanism for protecting IP and IPv6 traffic. Because BGP configuration requires explicitly configuring peer routers, it is quite feasible to set up IPSec security associations for the BGP traffic. Because IPSec key management can use secret passwords or public key certificates, IPSec offers very good scalability.

The GTSM has the lowest overhead of the three mechanisms, and is the easiest to configure. It also offers the least effective protection. The MD5 Signature mechanism offers low overhead and effective protection, but it forces administrators to disrupt their BGP sessions at each key update, and it does not scale well. IPSec offers the most effective protection, least disruption, and best scalability. It also imposes the highest overhead (although the overhead is still small), and it is the most complex mechanism to configure.

The sub-sections below show how to configure BGP MD5 Signatures and IPSec for BGP. Because it is subsumed by the other two mechanisms, GTSM is not shown, consult section 4.4.5 of the RSCG for an example of configuring GTSM on IOS [41]. The examples show the configuration of router North, peering to an IPv6 router belonging to a network service provider. (The BGP configuration for a transit router would be much more complicated.)

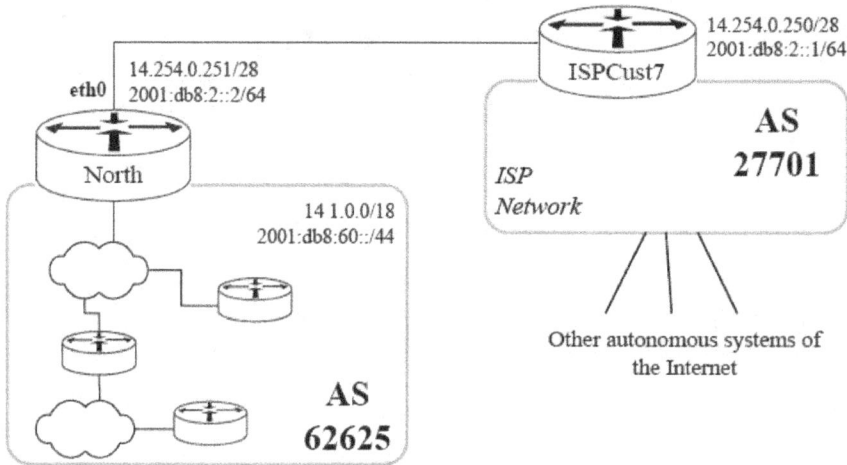

Figure 24: Example BGP Configuration

(Figure 24 shows an eBGP peering relationship. It is conventional to configure eBGP peering using physical interfaces. Large networks may use iBGP peering to convey external routes among their external BGP peering routers. It is conventional to configure iBGP using the loopback (lo0) interface, to improve consistency and uniformity of BGP setup across different hardware configurations.)

Configuring Multi-protocol BGP with MD5 Signatures

Before configuring MD5 signatures for BGP, you must select or obtain the secret password to be configured on each peer. For iBGP, the network security officer or designated administrator can select a secret. For BGP peering with another organization, you may need to negotiate selection procedures; some service providers may simply assign a secret to customers. It is also important to establish policies and procedures for when the secret will be changed, both periodically and in the event of compromise. Some of the recommendations in this section are based on the Team Cymru Secure BGP Template [60].

Configuring a BGP peering relationship to pass IPv4 and IPv6 routes over an IPv6 connection requires six main steps.

1. Create an IPv6 route-map to designate the next hop for IPv6 traffic, and an IPv6 prefix-list to restrict what IPv6 routes get announced to the external BGP. A prefix-list is not usually needed for iBGP, but is recommended for external BGP peering relationships.

2. Create an IPv4 route-map to designate the next hop for IPv4 traffic, and an IPv4 prefix-list to restrict what IPv4 routes get announced to the external BGP.

3. Set up the basic parameters for the BGP neighbor: the local router ID, local and remote AS numbers, the secret password, and any other BGP settings. Keep the neighbor relationship disabled until configuration is complete.

4. Configure the BGP neighbor relationship for the IPv4 address family.

5. Configure the BGP neighbor relationship for the IPv6 address family.

6. Enable the neighbor relationship.

Creating the prefix-lists and route-map are not very hard for a simple BGP relationship. For the prefix-list, we restrict the outgoing announcements to our allocated IPv4 and IPv6 address ranges. For the route-map, we only need to specify the next-hop addresses.

```
config t
! Route-map for designating IPv6 next hop
route-map bgp-27701-6map
  set ipv6 next-hop 2001:db8:2::2
  exit
! IPv6 prefix-list for filtering BGP announcements
ipv6 prefix-list bgp-out6 description BGP
          advertised routes for IPv6
ipv6 prefix-list bgp-out6 seq 10 permit
          2001:db8:60::/44
ipv6 prefix-list bgp-out6 seq 20 deny ::/0 le 128

! Route-map for designating IPv4 next hop
route-map bgp-27701-4map
  set ip next-hop 14.254.0.251
  exit
! IPv4 prefix-list for filtering BGP announcements
ip prefix-list bgp-out4 description BGP
          advertised routes for IPv4
ip prefix-list bgp-out4 seq 10 permit 14.1.0.0/18
ip prefix-list bgp-out4 seq 20 deny 0.0.0.0/0 le 32
```

In order for BGP to correctly advertise our allocated (aggregate) address blocks, IOS must know of routes to those exact blocks. Therefore, we may need to create static routes for those ranges.

```
! static routes for allocated address ranges
ipv6 route 2001:db8:60::/44 null0 254
ip route 14.1.0.0 255.255.192.0 null0 254
```

Setting up the basic parameters requires that we have selected the secret password to be used to protect the integrity of the BGP session, as well as the basic information about the peer router: AS number and interface address. Note that we disable the neighbor at this point; we'll enable it after the IPv6 and IPv4 address families are fully configured.

```
router bgp 62625
 bgp router-id 14.254.0.251
 neighbor 2001:db8:2::1 remote-as 27701
 neighbor 2001:db8:2::1 shutdown
 neighbor 2001:db8:2::1 0 dftuarmfIPv6nh
 bgp log-neighbor-changes
 no bgp fast-external-fallover
```

Configuring the IPv4 and IPv6 address families can be complicated, depending on your routing architecture. The example below shows how to apply the route-map and prefix-lists created in steps 1 and 2.

```
 address-family ipv6
  neighbor 2001:db8:2::1 activate
  neighbor 2001:db8:2::1 route-map
   bgp-27701-6map out
  neighbor 2001:db8:2::1 prefix-list
   bgp-out6 out
  network 2001:db8:60::/44
 exit-address-family

 address-family ipv4
  neighbor 2001:db8:2::1 activate
  neighbor 2001:db8:2::1 route-map
   bgp-27701-4map out
  neighbor 2001:db8:2::1 prefix-list
   bgp-out4 out
  network 14.1.0.0 255.255.192.0
 exit-address-family
```

Finally, we can enable the peering relationship.

```
  no neighbor 2001:db8:2::1 shutdown
 exit
exit
```

If the configuration is correct, and the peer router is ready, then the BGP adjacency should begin to come up within a few seconds. You can examine the relationship using the `show bgp` command.

```
        show bgp summary
                                                                    
                                                                    
    
    
                                                    /
                                      
        
```

IPSec for BGP

IPSec can defend BGP against direct integrity and denial-of-service attacks. Setting up IPSec in transport mode between two BGP peers is a little complex, but offers the strongest protection.

It is fairly easy to configure an IOS router to protect BGP with IPSec.

- If you are distributing both IPv4 and IPv6 BGP routes over an IPv4 BGP session, you can protect the session with IPv4 IPSec. Examples of configuring IPv4 IPSec appear in Section 4.2.2 of this document (p. 98), in Section 5.2 of the RSCG [41], and in many Cisco IOS security documents.

- If you are running distributing routes over an IPv6 BGP session, you can protect that session with IPSec. An example of configuring IPv6 IPSec appear in Section 4.2.1 of this document (p. 93).

A Final Word About BGP Security

The measures described above merely protect the integrity and reliability of a single BGP peering session. They cannot protect your network from the effects of inaccurate or malicious routes distributed through the BGP infrastructure.

BGP best practices for IPv6 are still evolving. This sub-section does not cover everything you may need to maintain a stable and reliable Internet BGP peer. IOS can perform route flap dampening, and it can enforce a variety of restrictions on the prefixes it accepts over BGP sessions. BGP can also be used to control defenses against some network denial-of-service attacks. For more information, consult sections 4.4.5 - 4.4.8 of the RSCG, and the book *ISP Essentials* [8].

If per-session integrity measures were adopted throughout the Internet, then the BGP infrastructure could gain significant protection against external attack. A malicious or mis-configured network provider could still disrupt routing by advertising routes they do not own. Ultimately, the Internet will need some form of hierarchical authorization system and associated security protocol for protecting BGP; at least one such scheme has already been standardized, but has not gained much acceptance.

4.2. IPSec and IPv6

IP Security (IPSec) is a suite of protocol extensions for IPv4 and IPv6 that provides integrity and confidentiality protection for network traffic. There are two IPSec protocols, both usable with IPv6:

- Authentication Header (AH) – this IPSec protocol uses hashed message authentication codes (HMAC) to provide integrity assurance.

- Encapsulated Security Payload (ESP) – this IPSec protocol uses encryption and HMAC to provide confidentiality and integrity assurance.

The Internet Key Exchange (IKE) protocol provides secure authentication and key management for IPSec. The IPv6 standards require that IPv6-capable nodes implement IPSec, but it does not require them to support IKE.

Because it operates at layer 3, IPSec can be applied in a wide variety of ways: protecting traffic between hosts, from remote hosts to home networks, between sites, between routers, and even traffic in tunnels. This section will present two general usage scenarios for IPSec and IKE:

1. Site-to-site VPN – protect all IPv6 traffic between two trusted networks, where the traffic must travel over an untrusted network.

2. Secure Configured Tunnel – protect IPv6 traffic being tunneled over an untrusted IPv4 network.

IPSec can also be used to protect control plane functions, such as routing protocols or IPv6 mobility registration messages. Section 4.1 shows an example of using IPSec AH to protect OSPFv3.

For general information about IPSec and its use with Cisco IOS, consult the Cisco IPSec introduction white paper [55]. For deep technical details about IPSec and IKE, consult Doraswamy and Harkins' book on IPSec [56].

IPv6 IPSec Support in IOS

Cisco IOS supports IPSec for IPv6 in releases 12.3 and later, but supports IKE for IPv6 only in releases 12.4(4)T and later. This means that only IOS 12.4(4)T and later can be used as a full IPv6 VPN gateway. (In addition to the right version you must also install the right IOS feature set.) Because earlier IOS releases do not support the key management functions of IKE, they cannot be used for site-to-site IPv6 VPNs. For more details about which IOS releases support particular features, consult [43].

The IOS releases that do support IKE for IPv6 support several different mechanisms for IKE authentication: pre-shared key, RSA key encryption, and RSA signature. The process for setting up the RSA-based methods is very complex; this document covers only the easier but less scalable pre-shared key mechanism. It is important to note that the security of the pre-shared key mechanism depends on the secrecy of that key – choose a long and complicated key, and protect it. If possible, obtain a PKI certificate for your routers, and use the RSA signature mechanism instead. For complete information about the IKE PKI features of IOS consult the IOS 12.4 Configuration Guide and [58].

4.2.1. Configuring an IPv6 Site-to-Site VPN

This sub-section presents an extended example of setting up IPSec to protect IPv6 traffic between the router North and the router Remote. This example uses IPv6 exclusively, and provides only brief explanations of the rationale behind each step of the process. Section 5.2 of the RSCG [41] presents a similar example for IPv4, with much more detailed explanations.

This example uses the Cisco IPSec "Virtual Tunnel Interface" (VTI) approach. We will set up an IPSec-protected tunnel between North and Remote. Figure 25 shows the interfaces and addresses.

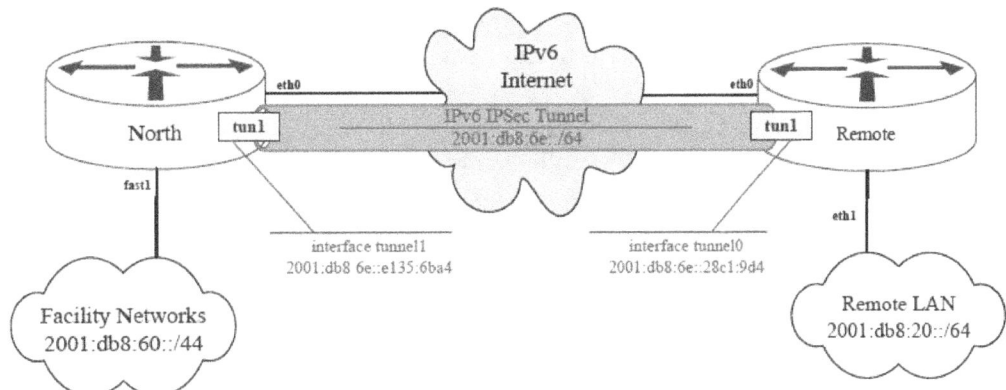

Figure 25: Site-to-Site IPv6 VPN Tunnel Example

Configuration Steps

Configuring site-to-site protection for IPv6 can be done in seven steps, listed below. The steps must be performed on each router (North and Remote).

1. Define an IKE policy – Cisco IOS uses the keyword "isakmp" for all IKE configuration commands (ISAKMP is a foundational protocol that was part of the basis for IKE). Use the command `crypto isakmp policy` to define a policy.

2. Set an IKE pre-shared key – set the same key on each router, associated with the IPv6 address of the peer router.

3. Configure an IPSec transform set and profile – select hash and cipher algorithms and parameters. You can set up several different transform

sets and profiles, but the two peers must have a set in common or they will not be able to communicate. For a site-to-site VPN, it is best to configure both peers with exactly the desired protection settings.

4. Configure an IKE (ISAKMP) profile – select the mechanism used to authenticate the peers to each other.

5. Define access lists – create access lists to restrict the traffic that can travel through the tunnel.

6. Create and configure the Virtual Tunnel Interface (VTI) – create a tunnel interface, and configure it to use the IKE and IPSec settings entered in steps 1-4, and the ACL entered in step 5.

7. Add routes – to force traffic to use the tunnel, and benefit from its protection, add one or more static routes to each router that designate the tunnel as the best path to the peer site's network, or set up dynamic routing using a routing protocol.

The transcripts below show the full configuration for router North. For steps where the configurations for North and Remote differ, both are shown.

Step 1: IKE Policy

The ISAKMP policy designates algorithms and cryptographic parameters for the IKE negotiations. The example below shows recommended settings.

```
config t
crypto isakmp policy 10
  encryption aes
  authentication pre-share
  group 5
  lifetime 43200
  exit
```

Step 2: IKE Pre-shared Key

In this step, we set the pre-shared authentication key that North and Remote will use to authenticate to each other during the IKE negotiations. Each router must be configured with the same key, but the configuration statement must designate the address of the appropriate interface on the peer router. For North, we use Remote's IPv6 Internet address:

```
crypto isakmp key gvn8cap800-900
        address ipv6 2001:db8:2f::2/128 no-xauth
```

And for Remote, we must use North's address:

```
crypto isakmp key gvn8cap800-900
        address ipv6 2001:db8:6f::2/128 no-xauth
```

These keys are placed in the default ISAKMP keyring. IOS supports multiple named keyrings, which should be used when the router is hosting remote client VPN services for multiple different groups of clients.

Step 3: IPSec Transform Set and Profile

The IPSec transform set is a named group of IPSec cryptographic settings. For this example, we will define only one transform set, using AES for confidentiality and SHA-1 HMAC for integrity. We also stipulate tunnel mode IPSec, which is necessary for a site-to-site VPN tunnel.

```
                    crypto ipsec transform-set
                        aesSet1 esp-sha-hmac esp-aes 128
                                    mode tunnel
                                    exit
```

Next, we set up the IPSec profile, which we need to bind the transform set to the tunnel interface in step 6.

```
                    crypto ipsec profile aesProfile1
                        description Strong VPN profile using AES
                        set transform-set aesSet1
                        exit
```

Step 4: ISAKMP Profile

The ISAKMP profile designates the identities of the two peers. North and Remote must have mirror configurations for the ISAKMP profile. The keyring must be explicitly designated; in this case we use the "default" keyring.

```
                    crypto isakmp profile ikeProfile1
                        description North-Remote profile
                        self-identity address ipv6
                        match identity address
                            ipv6 2001:db8:2f::2/128
                        keyring default
                        exit
```

And for Remote, we must use North's address:

```
                    crypto isakmp profile ikeProfile1
                        description Remote-North profile
                        self-identity address ipv6
                        match identity address
                            ipv6 2001:db8:6f::2/128
                        keyring default
                        exit
```

Step 5: Define ACLs

It is a good idea to impose traffic filtering at each tunnel endpoint, to ensure that only authorized traffic passes through the tunnel. In this example, the site-to-site VPN is authorized to carry all traffic between the two IPv6 networks, so the access lists can be fairly simple. The example ACLs below restrict the tunnel to carrying traffic between the two peer networks only.

For North:

```
                      ipv6 access-list vpn1-inbound-acl
                             permit ipv6 2001:db8:20::/64
                                         2001:db8:60::/44
                             permit ipv6 2001:db8:6e::/64
                                         2001:db8:60::/44
                             deny ipv6 any any log-input
                             exit

                      ipv6 access-list vpn1-outbound-acl
                             permit ipv6 2001:db8:60::/44
                                         2001:db8:20::/64
                             permit ipv6 2001:db8:60::/44
                                         2001:db8:6e::/64
                             exit
```

For Remote:

```
                      ipv6 access-list vpn1-inbound-acl
                             permit ipv6 2001:db8:60::/44
                                         2001:db8:20::/64
                             permit ipv6 2001:db8:60::/44
                                         2001:db8:6e::/64
                             deny ipv6 any any log-input
                             exit

                      ipv6 access-list vpn1-outbound-acl
                             permit ipv6 2001:db8:20::/64
                                         2001:db8:60::/44
                             permit ipv6 2001:db8:6e::/64
                                         2001:db8:60::/44
                             exit
```

Step 6: Tunnel Interface

Finally, we can set up the IPSec VTIs on each router. The configurations are nearly identical on North and Remote, because we have given the IPSec profiles and ACLs the same names.

```
                   interface tunnel1
                      ipv6 address 2001:db8:6e::e135:6ba4/64
                      ipv6 enable
                      ipv6 traffic-filter vpn1-inbound-acl in
                      ipv6 traffic-filter vpn1-outbound-acl out
                      tunnel source 2001:db8:6f::2
                      tunnel destination 2001:db8:2f::2
                      tunnel mode ipsec ipv6
                      tunnel protection ipsec profile aesProfile1
```

```
                       exit
```

And on Remote, merely different addresses:

```
                       interface tunnel1
                       ipv6 address 2001:db8:6e::28c1:9d4/64
                       ipv6 enable
                       ipv6 traffic-filter vpn1-inbound-acl in
                       ipv6 traffic-filter vpn1-outbound-acl out
                       tunnel source 2001:db8:2f::2
                       tunnel destination 2001:db8:6f::2
                       tunnel mode ipsec ipv6
                       tunnel protection ipsec profile aesProfile1
                       exit
```

Step 7: Add Routes

Once the tunnel is in place, we must set up static routes to make the tunnel the best path to the remote site network. On router North:

```
                 ipv6 route 2001:db8:20::/64
                       2001:db8:6e::28c1:9d4  10
                 exit
```

And on router Remote:

```
                 ipv6 route 2001:db8:60::/44
                       2001:db8:6e::e135:6ba4  10
                 exit
```

Verifying Operation of the Site-to-Site VPN

The IKE negotiations to set up the IPSec protection will not occur until the first time traffic is sent through the tunnel. To force this to occur, ping through the tunnel from one of the routers.

```
           ping ipv6 2001:db8:6e::28c1:9d4
```

You can check that IPSec status using various `show crypto` commands.

```
           show crypto ipsec sa
```

```
            □
              □
  □□□□□□□ □□□ □□□□
     □□□□ □□□□□□□□□□□□□□□□□□□□□□□□□□
        □□□□□□□□□□ □□□□□□□ □□□□□□□□□□□□ □
        □□ □□□ □□□□□□□□ □{□□□□□□□ }
      □
        □
  □□□□□□□□□ □□□ □□□□
     □□□□ □□□□□□□□□□□□□□□□□□□□□□□□□□
        □□□□□□□□□□ □□□□□□□ □□□□□□□□□□□□ □
        □□ □□□ □□□□□□□□ □{□□□□□□□ }
      □
        □
  □□□□□□□□ show crypto isakmp sa
  □□□□ □□□□□□□ □□□□□□ □□
  □□□              □□□        □□□□□□      □□□□□□□□ □□□□   □□□□□□□

  □□□□ □□□□□□□ □□□□□□ □□

   □□□□ □□□□□□□□□□□□□□□□□
   □□□□ □□□□□□□□□□□□□□□□□
   □□□□□□ □□□□□□□    □□□□□□□□ □□□□  □□□□□ □  □□□□□□□ □□□□□□

  □□□□□□□□ show crypto engine connection active
  □□□□□□□ □□□□□□ □□□□□□□□□□□
    □□ □□□□□□□□□ □□□□  □□□□□□□□□  □□□□□□□ □□□□□□□ □□□□□□□□□□
     □ □□□      □□□□□ □□□□□□□        □       □□ □□□□□□□□□□□□□□
     □□ □□□     □□□□□ □□□□□□□        □□       □ □□□□□□□□□□□□□□
    □□□□ □□□     □□□   □□□□□□□        □        □ □□□□□□□□□□□□□□

   □□□□□□□
```

For more information about IPSec configuration and status commands, consult the *IOS Security Command Reference* [58].

4.2.2. Using IPv4 IPSec to Protect IPv6 Tunnels

IPv6-capable versions of IOS prior to 12.4T support IPv6 tunnels, but do not support the encrypted IPv6 virtual tunnel interface shown above in Section 4.2.1. Many of those versions do support full IKE and IPSec for IPv4. This section shows how to use IPv4 IPSec to protect a manually configured IPv6 over a GRE tunnel. The example is shown in very terse form, for much more detailed explanations of all the IPv4 IPSec configuration commands, consult Section 5.2 of the RSCG [41].

Configuration Sequence

To configure an IPv6 tunnel with IPv4 IPSec protection, follow the steps in the following list for each of the tunnel endpoint routers. (Note: in this example, we use GRE for the tunnel encapsulation. The same approach will also work for simple IPv6 in IPv4 encapsulation as described in Section 3.6.1.)

1. Create IPv4 access lists that precisely match the IPv4 description of the tunnel traffic: protocol 47, and source and destination IPv4 tunnel endpoint addresses. (If using simple IPv6 over IPv4 tunneling, the protocol number would be 41.)

2. Configure an IKE pre-shared key and IKE policy using the `crypto isakmp` command.

3. Define an IPSec encryption transform set, using the command `crypto ipsec transform-set`.

4. Configure an IPSec crypto map, using the command `crypto map`.

5. Apply the IPSec crypto map to the tunnel source interface.

6. Configure the manual tunnel interface itself.

This approach works on a wide variety of IOS releases 12.3 and later.

Configuration Example

The example below shows how to configure a manual IPv6 over IPv4 tunnel with IPSec protection. The tunnel and addresses we will use are those shown in Section 3.6.1, (page 67). The steps show the configuration for router A; the steps for router B are the same but use router A's address.

Step 1, create IPv4 access lists that will match the tunnel traffic. Because the tunnel packets will be IPv6 encapsulated in IPv4 GRE, the access list must match on protocol 47. (If you use a simple IPv6 in IPv4 tunnel instead, replace 47 with 41.)

```
no access-list 159
access-list 159 permit 47 host 14.2.0.10
        host 7.12.1.11
access-list 159 permit 47 host 7.12.1.11
        host 14.2.0.10
```

Steps 2, configure the IKE policy and pre-shared key.

```
crypto isakmp policy 10
  encrypt aes 128
  authentication pre-share
  group 5
  exit
crypto isakmp key a8V9-Qx37u address 7.12.1.11
```

Steps 3 and 4, configure the IPSec transform set and IPSec crypto map.

```
crypto ipsec transform-set aes-esp-transform
        esp-aes esp-sha-hmac
  mode transport
  exit
crypto map protect-ipv6-tunnel 10 ipsec-isakmp
```

```
                                  set peer 7.12.1.11
                                  set transform-set aes-esp-transform
                                  match address 159
                                  exit
```

Step 5, apply the IPSec crypto map to the local interface that will serve as the source for the tunnel.

```
              interface ser0
              no crypto map
              crypto map protect-ipv6-tunnel
              exit
```

Finally, step 6, create the tunnel interface with its IPv6 address. You can use a GRE tunnel as shown here, or a simple IPv6-in-IPv4 tunnel (`mode ipv6ip`).

```
              interface tunnel0
              no ip address
              ipv6 address 2001:db8:ff::a/64
              ipv6 enable
              tunnel mode gre ip
              tunnel destination 7.12.1.11
              tunnel source 14.2.0.10
              end
```

After completing all these steps, the first packet through the tunnel will cause the two routers to perform their IKE negotiations and create IPSec security associations. IPv6 traffic through the tunnel will be protected with IPSec, transparently.

To confirm that the tunnel was set up correctly, use the command `ping` to force IPSec setup, and then use the command `show crypto ipsec` as illustrated below.

```
         ping 2001:db8:ff::b

                                         
         show crypto ipsec sa peer 7.12.1.11
```

```
#send errors 3, #recv errors 0

routerA#
```

For more information about configuring IPSec for IPv4, consult the Cisco IOS *Security Configuration Guide*.

4.3. Using the IOS Firewall for IPv6

IOS images that include the advanced security or advanced enterprise feature sets can serve as simple stateful inspection firewalls. While IOS routers do not offer all the features of a dedicated IPv6 firewall, they can provide firewall functionality for small networks or for deployments where a dedicated IPv6 firewall is not yet available. This section provides a short introduction to the IOS firewall features for IPv6.

In addition to the packet filtering offered by access lists, the IOS Firewall provides the following features:

- stateful inspection and filtering of TCP, UDP, ICMP, and FTP sessions,

- fragmented packet inspection, and

- mitigation for some denial-of-service attacks (e.g. TCP half-open connection flooding).

When it was first added to IOS, the firewall functionality was called Context-Based Access Control (CBAC). Some Cisco documentation still uses that name.

4.3.1. How the IOS Firewall Works

Figure 26 shows a simplified view of how the IOS firewall works. This simple usage scenario inspects traffic from the trusted network to the untrusted network (1), builds a state table for each outbound connection (2), and modifies the access list restricting traffic from the untrusted network to permit the corresponding inbound traffic (3).

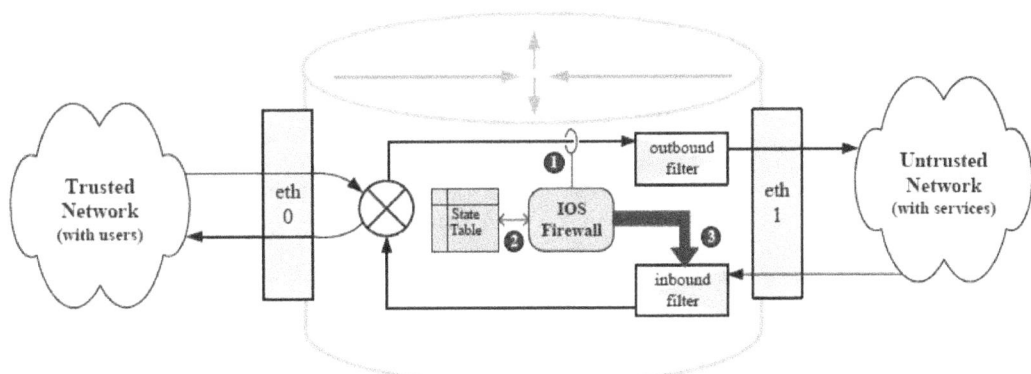

Figure 26: Operation of the IOS Firewall

The figure shows the IOS Firewall applied to traffic on Ethernet interfaces, but it works for any kind of interface, including tunnels. This means that you can use IOS Firewall protections for IPv6 tunnel traffic, as long as the tunnel terminates at the router (e.g. Sections 3.6.1 and 4.2.2). Of course, the IOS firewall is capable of managing connections in any direction through a router. For simplicity, only one direction is shown in the figure.

4.3.2. Checking for IOS Firewall Support

Only IOS images 12.3T and later that include the advanced security or advanced enterprise feature sets provide IOS Firewall capabilities. To check whether a router supports the IOS Firewall, use the command `show ipv6 inspect interfaces`.

Firewall Not Supported	Firewall Supported
▯▯▯▯▯ `show ipv6 inspect inter` ▯ ▯ ▯▯▯▯▯▯▯ ▯▯▯▯▯ ▯▯▯▯▯▯▯▯▯▯ ▯▯▯▯▯	▯▯▯▯▯▯ `show ipv6 inspect inter` ▯▯▯▯▯▯

If you need the Firewall capabilities but your IOS image does not support them, download and install one that does (see Section 3.1).

4.3.3. Configuring the IOS Firewall

To configure the IOS Firewall capabilities on a border router, you must configure and apply access lists to block traffic into the network. The IOS Firewall will very selectively permit traffic into the network, to allow sessions initiated by hosts inside the network. You may also configure a variety of IOS Firewall operational and logging parameters.

Basic Configuration

The basic structure for configuring the IOS Firewall is the named inspection rule set. You assign inspection rules to a set and apply the set to an interface using its name. Some default operational parameters for the Firewall, such a TCP timeouts, may be configured globally.

Use the `ipv6 inspect` command in configuration mode to add rules to an inspection list. The syntax is shown below.

```
ipv6 inspect name inspection-set-name protocol
     [ alert on|off ] [ audit-trail on|off ] [ timeout sec ]
```

The *protocol* field must be one of the following: `tcp`, `udp`, `icmp`, or `ftp`.

You must add a rule for each protocol you wish to manage through the firewall.

The **alert, audit-trail**, and **timeout** clauses on an inspection rule allow you to override the IOS Firewall global configuration for a specific rule. The **alert** and

audit-trail keywords control generation of IOS Firewall alert and audit messages. They allow you to override the default logging behavior. Logging is important for the overall security of a firewall, and should always be enabled by default; you can use "audit-trail off" to disable logging for a particular protocol if it is audited sufficiently elsewhere in your network. The **timeout** keyword allows you to override the default session timeout.

The line below shows how to add rules for inspecting UDP traffic and ICMP traffic.

```
South(config)# ipv6 inspect name FW-Ex1 udp timeout 15
South(config)# ipv6 inspect name FW-Ex1 icmp audit-trail off
```

Port-to-Application Mapping

The IOS Firewall inspects certain TCP and UDP ports for particular protocols and services. This is called Port-to-Application Mapping (PAM). IOS includes a basic set of mappings, associating each supported protocol with its default port. You can use the `ipv6 port-map` command to assign additional ports for supported protocols. The syntax for the command is shown below.

```
ipv6 port-map service-name port port-number [list acl-name]
```

The supported service names include http, smtp, ftp, h323, msrpc, sunrpc, and many others (see [44] for a list). Used without an ACL, this command sets a general mapping for the IOS firewall; used with an ACL, it sets a mapping that will apply only to traffic that matches the ACL.

For example, if your mail server needs to communicate with another mail server on non-standard port 2505, you can define that particular case as SMTP using an access list and a port mapping. The transcript below shows how to do this.

```
South(config)# ipv6 access-list MTAacl
South(config-ipv6-acl)# permit any host 2001:db9:6f:1::311
South(config-ipv6-acl)# exit
South(config)# ipv6 port-map smtp port 2505 list MTAacl
South(config)#
```

Use the command `show ipv6 port-map` to list the port-to-application mapping table. It will display both the system default mappings and any custom mappings you have defined.

Firewall Parameters

There a several operational parameters you may need to configure when applying the IOS Firewall.

Parameter Name	Default	Remarks
audit-trail	disabled	Logging is important for a firewall; enable audit-trail globally, and disable for specific protocols only when necessary. Enable as shown in the example, below.
max-incomplete-high	500	These two threshold control one aspect of the

Parameter Name	Default	Remarks
max-incomplete-low	400	Firewall's DoS mitigation. If the number of half-open sessions exceeds the -high mark, then the Firewall will start deleting sessions to defend the network from a flooding attack. Defensive behavior stops when the number drops below the -low mark. For busy networks, you may have to raise the values.
TCP idle-time	3600 sec.	This is the length of time that the IOS Firewall will maintain the state table entry for a TCP session with no traffic. The default value is one hour, for most networks, reduce it to 20 or 30 minutes.
TCP synwait-time	30 sec.	This is the length of time the Firewall will wait for a half-open connection to be completed. For fast networks, reduce to 15 sec.; for slow or highly congested networks, increase to 60 sec.
UDP idle-time	30 sec.	This is the length of time the Firewall will maintain a UDP "session" with no traffic. For slow or highly congested networks, increase to 60 sec.

The IOS Firewall has several other parameters which you should not need to adjust; for details consult the *IOS IPv6 Command Reference* [44].

IOS Firewall Example

The example below shows how to configure the IOS Firewall on the router South. Because South serves two networks, all the Firewall configuration will be applied to its single 'upstream' interface, eth0. The Firewall configuration will enforce the following policy:

- All hosts are allowed to communicate via TCP and UDP to the DNS servers on the facility network, 2001:db8:60::/64.

- Hosts on LAN 3 (2001:db8:63::/64) are allowed to use all TCP services, all UDP services, and all ICMP services.

- Hosts on LAN 4 (2001:db8:64::/64) are allowed to use TCP for SSH, HTTP, and HTTPS only (ports 22, 80, and 443), and all ICMP services.

- In addition to rules for LAN 3 and LAN 4, the policy must allow IPv6 SSH from the Admin LAN to the router itself, and it must allow the router to participate in OSPFv3.

South uses 2001:db8:62::48a5:b1d3/64 for interface eth0, and 2001:db8:6d::10a4:63f5/128 for interface loopback0.

First, set up the access lists.

```
South# config t
Enter configuration commands, one per line. End with CNTL/Z
```

```
South(config)# no ipv6 access-list FW1-out-acl
South(config)# ipv6 access-list FW1-out-acl
South(config-ipv6-acl)# remark TCP rules for LAN 3
South(config-ipv6-acl)# permit tcp 2001:db8:63::/64 any
South(config-ipv6-acl)# remark TCP rules for LAN 4
South(config-ipv6-acl)# permit tcp 2001:db8:64::/64 any eq 22
South(config-ipv6-acl)# permit tcp 2001:db8:64::/64 any eq www
South(config-ipv6-acl)# permit tcp 2001:db8:64::/64 any eq 443
South(config-ipv6-acl)# remark UDP rules for LAN 3
South(config-ipv6-acl)# permit udp 2001:db8:63::/64 any
South(config-ipv6-acl)# remark ICMP rules for LAN 3 and 4
South(config-ipv6-acl)# permit icmp 2001:db8:63::/64 any
South(config-ipv6-acl)# permit icmp 2001:db8:64::/64 any
South(config-ipv6-acl)# remark allow DNS to DNS server
South(config-ipv6-acl)# permit tcp any 2001:db8:60::/64 eq 53
South(config-ipv6-acl)# permit udp any 2001:db8:60::/64 eq 53
South(config-ipv6-acl)# remark allow usual IPv6 ND messages
South(config-ipv6-acl)# permit icmp any any nd-ns
South(config-ipv6-acl)# permit icmp any any nd-na
South(config-ipv6-acl)# remark deny all else and log violations
South(config-ipv6-acl)# deny ipv6 any any log
South(config-ipv6-acl)# exit
South(config)# no ipv6 access-list FW1-in-acl
South(config)# ipv6 access-list FW1-in-acl
South(config-ipv6-acl)# remark Rules for router traffic
South(config-ipv6-acl)# permit tcp any
                        host 2001:db8:62::48a5:b1d3 eq 22
South(config-ipv6-acl)# permit tcp any
                        host 2001:db8:6d::10a4:63f5 eq 22
South(config-ipv6-acl)# permit 89 fe80::/10 any
South(config-ipv6-acl)# remark Rules for necessary ICMP
South(config-ipv6-acl)# permit icmp any any packet-too-big
South(config-ipv6-acl)# permit icmp any any destination-unreach
South(config-ipv6-acl)# permit icmp any any parameter-problem
South(config-ipv6-acl)# permit icmp any any nd-na
South(config-ipv6-acl)# permit icmp any any nd-ns
South(config-ipv6-acl)# deny ipv6 any any log
South(config-ipv6-acl)# exit
South(config)#
```

Next, define the firewall inspection rule set.

```
South(config)# ipv6 inspect name FW1 tcp
South(config)# ipv6 inspect name FW1 udp
South(config)# ipv6 inspect name FW1 icmp
```

Third, set global firewall parameters.

```
South(config)# ipv6 inspect tcp idle-time 1800
South(config)# ipv6 inspect tcp synwait-time 15
South(config)# no ipv6 inspect alert-off
South(config)# ipv6 inspect audit-trail
```

Last, apply the access lists and firewall rule set to the interface. Also, this interface should not be sending router advertisements because it will not act as a router for other hosts' traffic on LAN2. (In general, a router should not send router advertisements from an interface on which it is not prepared to offer general packet forwarding service.)

```
South(config)# interface eth0
South(config-if)# description External interface, southern net
South(config-if)# ipv6 traffic-filter FW1-out-acl out
South(config-if)# ipv6 traffic-filter FW1-in-acl in
South(config-if)# ipv6 inspect FW1 out
South(config-if)# ipv6 nd ra suppress
South(config-if)# end
South#
```

When the IOS Firewall inspection rule set is applied to the interface, as shown above, the outbound traffic from hosts on LAN 3 and LAN 4 will be inspected and corresponding return traffic will be permitted through the router.

For another example of configuring the IOS Firewall, see [47].

Monitoring Firewall Operation

To validate the IOS Firewall configuration, use the command `show ipv6 inspect` with a variety of options, as illustrated below.

```
South# show ipv6 inspect config
Session audit trail is enabled
Session alert is enabled
Routing Header inspection is disabled
one-minute (sampling period) thresholds are [400:500]
max-incomplete sessions thresholds are [400:500]
max-incomplete tcp connections per host is 50.
tcp synwait-time is 15 sec - tcp finwait-time is 5 sec
tcp idle-time is 1800 sec - udp idle-time is 30 sec
icmp idle-time is 10 sec
Session has table size is 1021
Inspection Rule Configuration
 Inspection name FW1
    icmp alert is on audit-trail is on timeout 10
    udp alert is on audit-trail is on timeout 30
    tcp alert is on audit-trail is on timeout 1800

South# show ipv6 inspect interfaces
Interface Configuration
 Interface Ethernet0
  Inbound inspection rule is not set
  Outgoing inspection rule is FW1
    icmp alert is on audit-trail is on timeout 10
    udp alert is on audit-trail is on timeout 30
    tcp alert is on audit-trail is on timeout 1800

South#
```

```
South# show ipv6 inspect sessions
Established Sessions
 Session 5681 (2001:64::3e)=>(2001:200:0:8000::42) tcp SIS-OPEN
 Session 57803 (2001:63::41f3)=>(2001:60::53) udp SIS-OPEN
     .
       .
South# show ipv6 port-map
Default mapping: dns       port 53          system defined
Default mapping: gtpv1     port 2123        system defined
Default mapping: vdolive   port 7000        system defined
Default mapping: sunrpc    port 111         system defined

     .
       .
Host specific:   smtp    port 2025  in list MTAacl user defined
     .
       .
South#
```

For more details about commands for examining the IOS Firewall, consult [44].

5. Emerging Issues

This short section describes a few emerging technologies that will have a profound effect on IPv6 network security. There are many such future concerns in the network area; the technologies discussed below were chosen because they directly concern IPv6 security and IPv6 routers.

5.1. Secure Neighbor Discovery and Cryptographically Generated Addresses

IPv6 links depend on correct operation of several control protocols, notably neighbor discovery, router discovery, and related schemes. In the core IPv6 standards, these protocols are defined as operating only on the local link, but without any kind of integrity protection. The lack of protection can leave IPv6 networks exposed to several different and fairly serious threats from hostile parties on the local link. These threats are described in RFC 3756 [26], and in a variety of other forums. Two representative ones are listed below.

- By using spoofed neighbor advertisements, a malicious host can masquerade as other hosts.

- By using spoofed router advertisements, a malicious host can deny service to hosts on the link, or act as a router for them and control all their traffic.

SEcure Neighbor Discovery (SEND) and Cryptographically Generated Addresses (CGA) are two IETF specifications designed to provide some integrity assurance for addresses and control protocols on IPv6 links. SEND is described in RFC 3971 [34], and CGA in RFC 3972 [35].

CGA

CGA is a specification for binding part of an IPv6 address to an RSA public key. A node that uses CGA must first possess, or generate, an RSA key pair. The node allocates a CGA by using the 64-bit network identifier (configured statically or obtained via auto-configuration) and 64 bits of a hash as the interface identifier. The hash must be computed over a CGA control structure that contains the network identifier, the public half of the RSA keypair, and other control information. The node can also sign assertions that it is the owner of the CGA, using the private half of the keypair.

With CGA, other nodes on the network can verify that that a node claiming an address is really the owner of that address by verifying a signature. CGA is a building block for securing control messages that depend on addresses. SEND provides assurance for neighbor discovery and router discovery partly by using CGA.

SEND

The base RFC that describes Neighbor Discovery (RFC 2461) recommends IPSec for protecting neighbor discovery messages. The RFC does not describe how to apply IPSec for this purpose, and the Internet community has come to the concensus that using IPSec in its current form is not practical for neighbor discovery.

SEND was developed to mitigate many of the threats to neighbor discovery, without requiring IPSec or extensive key management effort.

There are three main parts to the SEND specification:

- Certification of routers – the SEND specification describes how to certify routers with public key certificates, and how SEND-capable hosts can verify the authenticity of routers before depending on them for service.

- Cryptographically Generated Addresses – nodes use CGA to ensure that the sender of a ND message is really the owner of any address claimed in the message.

- New ND message options – the SEND specification defines three new ND options, and describes how they must be used in ND messages. The three options are:

  - RSA signature option, used for signing SEND messages,

  - the timestamp option, used for anti-replay protection on ND messages sent to multicast addresses, and

  - the nonce option, used for protecting solicitation-response message pairs.

While SEND cannot eliminate all risks from neighbor discovery, it can greatly reduce the scope of attacks and make detection of some attempted attacks easier. Some of the key benefits of SEND depend on provisioning routers with public key certificates.

SEND and CGA are not yet widely implemented. Once they are, configuring SEND on routers will be an important part of IPv6 security for local LANs.

5.2. IPv6 Host Mobility and Network Mobility

When a host connects to the IPv6 Internet via many different LANs, it will typically use a different address on each. This can disrupt operation of some applications on the host, particularly network servers. Mobile IPv6 is a standard means for hosts to connect using different addresses, but maintain a 'virtual' presence at their home address. In other words, it provides mobile hosts the ability to keep the same address, and enjoy uninterrupted service through that address, while moving around the IPv6 Internet. Nodes elsewhere on the network can send packets to the mobile host's home address, and the host can send and receive the packets wherever it is.

Mobile IPv6 (MIPv6) defines several terms that you must know before learning how it works or what security issues it poses.

- **Home Address** – the original or long-term address of a mobile host.

- **Home Agent** – a network node, usually a router, that can act as a proxy for the mobile host when it is using an address other than its home address.

- **Care-of Address** – an address used by a mobile host when it is attached to an access network other than its home network.

- **Correspondent Node** – any other IPv6 node on the network that communicates with the mobile host.

An explanation of relevant terms can be found in RFC 3775 [36]. Chapter 8 of *Deploying IPv6 Networks* provides extensive details on IPv6 mobility [9].

Operation of Mobile IPv6

IPv6 host mobility depends on a home agent, permanently attached to the mobile host's home network. When the mobile host is attached somewhere other than its home network, it registers its new address (the "care-of" address) with the home agent. The home agent acts as an intermediary or network-layer proxy, accepting packets on behalf of the mobile node, and forwarding them to the mobile node through a tunnel. The mobile node responds back through the tunnel, and the home agent sends forwards the packets to the correspondent node. This is called bidirectional tunneling or triangle routing. It works without the correspondent node or the access network needing any special software or settings. Figure 27 illustrates how the correspondent node, home agent, and mobile host communicate.

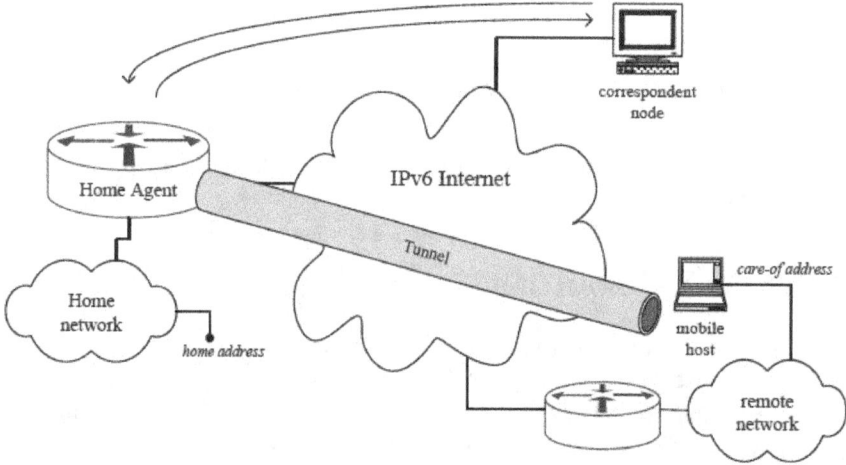

Figure 27: Bidirectional Tunneling for Mobile IPv6

Before the mobile host can communicate with any correspondent nodes using its home address, it must register a *binding* with the home agent. Integrity of the binding messages is critical to secure operation of MIPv6; the specification mandates use of IPSec to protect these messages (see RFC 3776).

Triangle routing works, but it is inefficient. Every packet traverses the network twice, and in particular traverses the link to the home agent twice. The Mobile IPv6 specification defines route optimization; using it, mobile hosts and correspondent nodes can communicate directly. Route optimization uses a complicated return routability procedure between the mobile node and correspondent node. It requires software support on both the mobile node and the correspondent node. For details of route optimization and the return routability procedure, consult RFC 3775 [36].

Some Security Implications of MIPv6

There are three network roles that matter when considering MIPv6 security:

- **Home network** – a network that supports home agents must permit binding messages and the special extension headers that support MIPv6, as well as the tunnel traffic between the mobile host and the home agent. This network accepts some risk, because it is essentially allowing the remote mobile host IPv6 access to the local LAN.

  The home agent itself must be configured to support mobile hosts, including IPSec security for binding.

- **Access network** – a network that allows mobile hosts must provide some facility to assign them addresses, and must permit the tunnel traffic between the mobile hosts and their home agents. To allow efficient service for mobile hosts, the access network must also allow the mobility extension header used for route optimization. The tunnel represents a particular risk, because the encapsulation may allow traffic to bypass the access network's boundary filtering. (For example, the ingress access list recommendation presented in Section 3.3.5 would not support mobile hosts, because it does not allow protocol 41.)

- **Correspondent network** – any IPv6 network should support correspondent nodes, especially if the network hosts any servers. Fortunately, the minimum requirement for supporting correspondent nodes is simply allowing type 2 routing extension headers. Supporting route optimization requires allowing the mobility extension header, too. Communicating with mobile hosts does not generally impose extra risk on correspondent nodes or their networks.

The newest versions of IOS provide access list capabilities for exercising more fine-grained control over the extension headers and ICMPv6 messages used for MIPv6.

It is important to note that IPv6 mobility offers a mobile host the ability to act as if it is attached to its home network, but does not force *all* of its communication through the home network. The mobile host can use its care-of address to communicate. In this sense, a mobile host gains full tunneled access into the home network, but also any exposure or risk of both the home network and the access network. Best practices in this area are still being discussed. It would be prudent to do a thorough risk analysis before configuring home agent support on your network.

Network Mobility (NEMO)

The IPv6 Mobility specification defines means for a single host to remain constantly connected on its home address as it moves around the IPv6 network. What if a whole network needs to move around? There are several situations where this can be very useful, two common ones are discussed below.

- Vehicle networks – a network on a car, truck, or ship can appear to be connected via its home address, even as it moves around and uses different access networks. The mobility is completely transparent for all the IPv6 hosts in the vehicle. For example, a ship might use local network services for access while docked in a foreign port, but remain reachable via its home address.

- Deployable networks – for disaster response, military operations, and other rapid deployments, it is helpful to keep a complete network configured, tested, and prepared. Using network mobilty, an entire network can be deployed and operated without any configuration changes, using any kind of connection.

The IPv6 Network Mobility (NEMO) specification, RFC 3963 [37], defines the operation of a mobile network router. By implementing the specification, a router can provide transparent connectivity (with no renumbering) for hosts and routers that belong to the mobile network. NEMO always uses bidirectional tunneling; all traffic to the mobile network must be forwarded through the home agent. At this time, there is no route optimization mechanism defined for mobile networks.

Security Implications of NEMO

Many of the security issues for NEMO are similar to those for host mobility, but without the considerations involving route optimization.

A mobile router must impose security policy on the mobile network. The point of NEMO is for traffic from hosts on the mobile network to work exactly as if the network was attached to its home connection. In addition to the general boundary filtering rules described in Section 3.3.5, a mobile router should enforce some specific mobility security policies.

- Packets for the mobile network must arrive on the tunnel from the home agent. Any non-tunnel packet arriving on the access link with a destination address in the mobile network must be dropped.

- A mobile router must not advertise routing services on the access link. It must not forward packets from outside the mobile network into the tunnel.

- All packets received from the nodes on the mobile network must have source addresses within the mobile network's allocated home prefixes. In particular, nodes on the mobile network must not be permitted to send packets as if they belonged to the access network.

- Mobile routers should not participate in dynamic routing protocols on the access network, though they may participate in dynamic routing on their home network via the home agent.

- IPSec must be configured between the home agent and the mobile router to protect binding messages. When possible, IPSec should be used to protect all traffic in the tunnel.

A home agent supporting a mobile network must also enforce some security rules, described in [37].

An access network configured to allow mobile hosts will also support mobile networks. The security concerns are roughly the same.

For details about host mobility support in IPv6, consult RFC 3775 [36]; network mobility is defined as an extension to host mobility; for details see RFC 3963 [37]. An example of configuring IPv6 mobility features in Cisco IOS appears in [9].

6. Conclusions

Security will be a serious concern for network administrators and users during the migration to IPv6. To make the security of our IPv6 networks even better than their IPv4 predecessors, we will need two things: security functions and features that work for IPv6, and standards and concensus practices on how to apply them.

Initially, we can approach IPv6 security by applying our existing security practices to the new protocol. This works well for many aspects of IPv6 router security, such as the examples below.

- Protect the integrity and confidentiality of management sessions – in IPv4 we can use SSH, SSL, and IPSec; these protocols work well for IPv6 too. Authentication methods are independent of the network protocols.

- Disable unnecessary management and control services – many of the same services need to be disabled for IPv4 and IPv6.

- Protect sensitive traffic between trusted partners – IPSec can be used for this purpose with both IPv4 and IPv6.

Some principles we apply for IPv4 apply to IPv6, but require slightly different implementations.

- Ensure the integrity and availability of routing protocols – most IPv4 routing protocols include a simple integrity mechanism. Some IPv6 routing protocols depend on IPSec instead.

- Block illicit and hostile traffic at network boundaries – the mechanisms we use to block undesired traffic are the same for IPv4 and IPv6: traffic filters and rate-limiting. The specific kinds of traffic we can filter, and the considerations for rate-limiting, differ considerably between IPv4 and IPv6.

Finally, a few new issues that we must face when deploying IPv6, especially during the transition period. Ensuring security for manual and automatic tunnels requires applying old mechanisms in new ways.

The network security and operations community has not yet settled on all the best practices for IPv6 networks. The worldwide migration to IPv6 is still in its early stages. Experts from industry, government, and academia need to work together to define security guidelines and standards, test them, and publish them. This document is a first attempt from a government viewpoint, but it is sure to change and evolve as IPv6 products and practices mature. The maturation process will include three parts.

1. Security and operations experts need to identify important security mechanisms for IPv6 and mixed IPv4/v6 networks.

2. Network vendors need to build those mechanisms into robust, efficient products.

3. Network operators and administrators need to apply the mechanisms, consistently and uniformly.

Securing our IPv6 routers is an important part in hardening our IPv6 networks, but it is only one step in many. This document illustrates the use of many security features of Cisco IOS routers. Those features are most effective when applied as part of a comprehensive security strategy.

7. References

Books

[1] Davies, J., *Understanding IPv6*, Microsoft Press, 2002.

A well-written and accessible introduction to IPv6, written from more of a host-oriented viewpoint.

[2] Desmeules, R., *Cisco Self-Study: Implementing Cisco IPv6 Networks*, Cisco Press, 2003.

A very detailed overview of IPv6, written from a network-oriented viewpoint. Provides instructions for configuring IPv6 functionality on Cisco routers.

[3] Hagen, S., *IPv6 Essentials*, O'Reilly, 2002.

Provides very good explanations of the protocol itself, neighbor discovery, routing, and transition mechanisms. Starting to get out of date in a few areas.

[4] Loshin, P., *IPv6: Theory, Protocol, and Practice, 2nd Edition*, Morgan Kaufmann, 2003.

Very detailed coverage of IPv6 issues, including some treatment of transition strategies and configuration on various platforms.

[5] Malone, D., *IPv6 Network Administration*, O'Reilly, 2005.

A highly practical and concrete introduction, written from a network-oriented viewpoint. Provides instructions for setting up IPv6 on several different platforms, including Cisco routers.

[6] Akin, T., *Hardening Cisco Routers*, O'Reilly, 2002.

This pragmatic book gives excellent advice on securing Cisco routers using IPv4. The principles it provides also apply to IPv6.

[7] van Beijnum, I. *Running IPv6*, Apress, 2006.

This fairly new book gives detailed information about IPv6 configuration on a wide variety of platforms, and includes discussion of many security issues.

[8] Greene, B. and Smith, P., *Cisco ISP Essentials*, 1st Edition, Cisco Press, April 2002.

This detailed Cisco guide for Internet Service Providers includes extensive discussion of routing protocols (especially BGP), and an in-depth treatment of Unicast RPF, all with fully worked-out examples.

[9]   Levy-Abegnoli, Popoviciu, and Grossetete, *Deploying IPv6 Networks*, Cisco Press, 2006.

> Fairly new book providing detailed guidance on planning, building, and operating IPv6 networks.

[10] Dunmore, M. (ed.), *6Net – An IPv6 Deployment Guide*, 6Net Consortium, 2005. available at: `http://www.6net.org/book/deployment-guide.pdf`

> A very extensive overview of IPv6 with detailed descriptions of deployment strategies and lessons learned.

RFCs and Internet-Drafts

RFCs may be obtained from `www.rfc-editor.org` and many other repositories. Internet drafts are works in progress, and change frequently; they may be obtained from `www.ietf.org` and other repositories.

[11] Deering, S. and Hinden, R., "Internet Protocol, Version 6 (IPv6) Specification", RFC 2460, December 1998.

> The core standard that defines the IPv6 address, packet header format, and fundamental extension headers.

[12] Conta, A. and Deering, S., "Internet Control Message Protocol (ICMPv6) for IPv6 Specification", RFC 2463, December 1998.

[13] Deering, S. and Hinden, R., "Internet Protocol, Version 6 (IPv6) Addressing Architecture", RFC 3513, April 2003.

[14] Narten, T., Nordmark, E., and Simpson, W., "Neighbor Discovery for IP Version 6 (IPv6)", RFC 2461, December 1998.

[15] Narten, T. and Thomson, S., "IPv6 Stateless Address Autoconfiguration", RFC 2462, December 1998.

[16] McCann, J., Deering, S., and Mogul, J., "Path MTU Discovery for IPv6", RFC 1981, August 1996.

[17] Gilligan, R, and Nordmark, E., "Basic Transition Mechanisms for IPv6 Hosts and Routers", RFC 4213, October 2005.

[18] Deering, S., Fenner, W., and Haberman, B. "Multicast Listener Discovery (MLD) for IPv6", RFC 2710, October 1999.

[19] Vida, R. and Costa, L. (ed.s), "Multicast Listener Discovery Version 2 (MLDv2) for IPv6", RFC 3810, June 2004.

[20] Malkin, G. and Minnear, R., "RIPng for IPv6", RFC 2080, January 1997.

[21] Bates, T., *et al*, "Multi-protocol Extensions for BGP-4", RFC 2858, June 2000.

[22] Coltun, R., Ferguson, D., and Moy, J., "OSPF for IPv6", RFC 2740, December 1999.

[23] Hopps, C.E., "Routing IPv6 with IS-IS", work in progress, October 2005.

[24] Ferguson, P. and Senie, D., "Network Ingress Filtering: Defeating Denial of Service Attacks which employ IP Source Address Spoofing", May 2000.

[25] Baker, F. and Savola, P., "Ingress Filtering for Multihomed Networks", RFC 3704, March 2004.

[26] Nikander, P., Kempf, J., and Nordmark, E., "IPv6 Neighbor Discovery (ND) Trust Models and Threats", RFC 3756, May 2004.

[27] Hinden, R. and Haberman, B., "Unique Local IPv6 Unicast Addresses", RFC 4193, October 2005.

[28] Davies, E., Krishnan, S., and Savola, P., "IPv6 Transition/Co-Existence Security Considerations", work in progress, July 2005.

[29] Van de Velde, G., *et al*, "IPv6 Network Architecture Protection", work in progress, June 2005.

[30] Davies, E. and Mohacsi, J., "Best Current Practices for Filtering ICMPv6 Messages in Firewalls", work in progress, July 2005.

[31] Tsirtsis, G. and Srisuresh, P., "Network Address Translation - Protocol Translation (NAT-PT)", RFC 2766, February 2000.

[32] Carpenter, B. and Moore, K., "Connection of IPv6 Domains over IPv4 Clouds", RFC 3056, February 2001.

[33] Murphy, S., "BGP Security Vulnerabilities Analysis", RFC 4272, January 2006.

[34] Arkko, Kempf, Zill, and Nikander, "SEcure Neighbor Discovery (SEND)", RFC 3971, March 2005.

[35] Aura, T., "Cryptographically Generated Addresses (CGA)", RFC 3972, March 2005.

[36] Johnson, D., Arkko, J., and Perkins, C., "Mobility Support in IPv6", RFC 3775, June 2004.

[37] Devarapalli, V. *et al*, "Network Mobility (NEMO) Basic Support Protocol", RFC 3963, January 2005.

Papers, Manuals, and Presentations

[38] Convery, S. and Miller, D., "IPv6 and IPv4 Threat Comparison and Best-Practice Evaluation", version 1.0, Cisco Systems, March 2004.
available at: http://www.cisco.com/security_services/ciag/documents/v6-v4-threats.pdf

> A seminal analysis of network risks posed by IPv6, and comparison with risks posed by IPv4. This paper also includes some security guidance for configuring Cisco routers.

[39] *The ABCs of IP Version 6*, Cisco Systems, July 2002.

> An early overview document from Cisco, provides a very good introduction to IPv6 in a network context.

[40] U.S. Government Accountability Office, "Internet Protocol Version 6 – Federal Agencies Need to Plan for Transition and Manage Security Risks", GAO Report GAO-05-471, May 2005.
available at: http://www.gao.gov/cgi-bin/getrpt?GAO-05-471

> This government report presents a high-level view of IPv6 transition.

[41] Ziring, N. (ed.), "Router Security Configuration Guide, version 1.1c, report number C4-040R-02, National Security Agency, December 2005.
available under: http://www.nsa.gov/snac/downloads_cisco.cfm

> NSA's security configuration guidance for Cisco IOS, covering general issues and IPv4.

[42] *Cisco IOS IPv6 Configuration Guide, Release 12.4T*, Cisco Systems, 2004.
available at:
http://www.cisco.com/application/pdf/en/us/guest/products/ps5187/c2001/ccmigration_09186a00801d7f16.pdf

> This is the official IOS 12.4T configuration manual for IPv6. The chapter "Implementing Security for IPv6" provides a great deal of useful information and configuration examples.

[43] "Start Here: Cisco IOS Software Release Specifics for IPv6 Features", Cisco IOS IPv6 Configuration Library, Cisco Systems, November 2005.
available at: http://www.cisco.com/univercd/cc/td/doc/product/software/ios123/123cgcr/ipv6_c/ftipv6s.pdf

> This chapter from the IOS 12.4 IPv6 documentation gives a long list of IPv6 features, and the IOS releases that support them.

[44] *Cisco IOS IPv6 Command Reference,* Cisco Systems, 2005.
available under: http://www.cisco.com/en/US/products/ps6350/
prod command reference list.html

> This is the official IOS 12.4 command reference for IPv6. It provides extensive detail on all IPv6 commands.

[45] Potyraj, C., "Security Analysis for DoD IPv6 Transition, Report 1: IPsec", National Security Agency, 2005.
available under: http://www.nsa.gov/ia/

> A deep analysis of IPSec security in the context of IPv6.

[46] "Cisco IOS Packaging: Products and Services", Cisco Systems, 2005.
available under:
http://www.cisco.com/en/US/products/sw/iosswrel/ps5460/

> An explanation of the unified scheme for IOS feature set naming.

[47] "Implementing Security for IPv6", *Cisco IOS IPv6 Configuration Library*, Cisco System, September 2005.
available under:
http://www.cisco.com/en/US/products/sw/iosswrel/ps5187/
products installation and configuration guides list.html

> This chapter of the IOS 12.3 Configuration Library provides good coverage of IPv6 access lists, and a listing of which security features are supported in which IOS releases.

[48] Garfinkel, S., "Internet 6.0", MIT Technology Review, January 2004.
available under:
http://www.technologyreview.com/articles/archive/

> An influential article that disparaged IPv6 for its potential impact on the speed and safety of the Internet; warns that eliminating widespread use of IPv4 NAT will be deleterious to enterprise security.

[49] "Unicast RPF for IPv6 on the Cisco 12000 Series", Cisco IOS 12.0S Release Notes, Cisco Systems, September 2005.
available at:
http://www.cisco.com/univercd/cc/td/doc/product/software/ios12
0/120newft/120limit/120s/120s31/urpf gsr.pdf

> This documentation note for the 12000 GSR provides a clear explanation of how uRPF works, along with usage recommendations and several examples.

[50] *Cisco IOS Quality of Service Solutions Configuration Guide*, Release 12.4, Cisco Systems, 2005.

> This is the detailed configuration guide for traffic shaping, rate limiting, policing, and related facilities. While the examples use IPv4, the concepts and most of the command syntax are identical for IPv6.

[51] "Quality of Service (QoS) Introduction", Cisco Systems, 2005.
available at:
`http://www.cisco.com/en/US/tech/tk543/tsd_technology_support_c ategory_home.html`

This portion of Cisco's web site provides papers, documentation, and other materials about QoS, traffic shaping, and related facilities.

[52] *Cisco IOS Quality of Service Command Reference*, Release 12.4, Cisco Systems, 2005.

This manual describes all the commands that comprise the QoS facility on IOS routers.

[53] "Control Plane Policing", *Cisco IOS Quality of Service Solutions Configuration Guide*, Release 12.4, Cisco Systems, 2005.
available at:
`http://www.cisco.com/univercd/cc/td/doc/product/software/ios12 4/124cg/hqos_c/part20/ch05/hrtlimt.pdf`

This chapter of the QoS Configuration Guide explains CPP in detail, with IPv4 examples.

[54] "Interconnecting IPv6 Domains Using Tunnels", Cisco Internetworking Technology white paper, Cisco Systems, 2003.
available at:
`http://www.cisco.com/univercd/cc/td/doc/cisintwk/intsolns/ ipv6_sol/v6domain.pdf`

This introductory paper presents some issues and approaches for connecting IPv6 networks over the IPv4 infrastructure.

[55] "An Introduction to IP Security (IPSec) Encryption", Cisco Technical Notes, Cisco Systems, May 2003.
available at: `http://www.cisco.com/warp/public/105/IPSECpart1.pdf`

This technical note offers a general overview of IPSec and some detailed information about Cisco IPSec support.

[56] Doraswamy, N. and Harkins, D., *IPSec: The New Security Standard for the Internet, Intranets, and Virtual Private Networks*, 2nd Edition, Prentice-Hall, 2003.

This book provides very detailed information about the IPSec and IKE protocols, but with an emphasis on IPv4.

[57] "Network Infrastructure Security Technical Information Guide", version 6 release 4, Defense Information Systems Agency, December 2005.
available under: `http://csrc.nist.gov/pcig/cig.html`

A detailed guide to secure network configuration with rationale and explicit directions. The examples use IPv4, but the principles are applicable to IPv6.

[58] *Cisco IOS Security Command Reference*, Release 12.4, Cisco Systems, 2005.
available at:
http://www.cisco.com/application/pdf/en/us/guest/products/
ps6350/c2001/ccmigration_09186a00804917ec.pdf

> This voluminous reference manual describes all the commands that support the AAA, IPSec and VPNs, AAA, firewall, IDS, CIPSO, and PKI facilities on IOS routers.

[59] Martey, A., *IS-IS Network Design Solutions*, Cisco Press, 2002.

> The definitive IS-IS reference and design guide; though it uses IPv4 for all the examples, it's principles and explanations are valuable for IPv6 too.

[60] Thomas, R., "Secure BGP Template Version 4.2", January 2006.
available at:
http://www.cymru.com/Documents/secure-bgp-template.html

> This short but highly prescriptive document gives a detailed example of a locked-down configuration for a backbone or border router using BGP-4. While it is specifically for IPv4, the principles it embodies are quite applicable to IPv6.

[61] "Implementing EIGRP for IPv6", Cisco Systems, 2006.
available at:
http://www.cisco.com/univercd/cc/td/doc/product/software/
ios123/123cgcr/ipv6_c/v6eigrp.pdf

> A short Cisco white paper describing EIGRP for IPv6 and giving directions on how to configure it.

8. Index